SIRETT PLAYS TWO

Paul Sirett

PLAYS TWO

WORLDS APART

CRUSADE

THIS OTHER EDEN

INTERNATIONAL CAFÉ

OBERON BOOKS

LONDON

First published in 2008 by Oberon Books Ltd
521 Caledonian Road, London N7 9RH
Tel: 020 7607 3637 / Fax: 020 7607 3629
e-mail: info@oberonbooks.com
www.oberonbooks.com

A catalogue record for this book is available from the British
Library.

ISBN: 978-1-84002-482-1

Cover photograph by Bartosz Hadyniak/www.stockexpert.com

Printed in Great Britain by CPI Antony Rowe, Chippenham

Contents

INTRODUCTION, 7

WORLDS APART, 11

CRUSADE, 71

THIS OTHER EDEN, 133

INTERNATIONAL CAFÉ, 199

Introduction

I directed *Worlds Apart* and *Crusade* at the Theatre Royal, Stratford East (TRSE). I talked to Paul about, and saw *This Other Eden.* I have to admit, I've only read *International Café.* However, I've recently worked with Paul, in Bangalore and London, on another play of his, *Bad Blood Blues* that I hope to direct soon, so I guess I'm qualified to comment...

In my introduction to his first collection of plays I mentioned our first meeting at the TRSE Writers Group I used to run. Our objective was always to involve writers in our theatrical process and Paul got engaged more than most, even running a project in a tough local school for us in very quick order.

From this involvement came the first play of Paul's I directed, *A Night in Tunisia.* After the success of this production (I seem to remember Lyn Gardner saying it made her cry) Paul and I began kicking ideas around for another play. At the time immigration policy was a hot topic (some things don't change). I was taking some Tibetan Buddhist instruction (I soon found it didn't really go with working in theatre, at least not for me) and Paul expressed an interest in Tibetan Opera (which I never did quite get). Thus arose *Worlds Apart*, a 'searing indictment' of the UK's immigration and political asylum policy based around a traditional Tibetan Opera plot... And it worked! Audiences loved it and we got one of the best set of national reviews I've personally ever had.

Trouble is, because it was seen as 'risky' it only got a very short run at Stratford East and has, to my knowledge, never been done again. The fate of far too many good 'new' plays I'm afraid.

We managed to get a fantastic cast together to do the show, many of whom have since gone on to great things in TV and movies, and Sue Mayes, the designer, came up with a great set that somehow managed to marry Heathrow Immigration with A Tibetan stupa.

I remember Paul and I making a pilgrimage to talk to a Tibetan musician who happened to be visiting Cambridge and eventually finding a video that enabled us to stage the Skeleton dances. Free Tibet were also a great help, and their T Shirts did a pretty good trade front-of-house in return (I've still got two).

The main thing for me about the play was how it managed to work, sometimes simultaneously, both on an everyday and a mythic basis. The extremely quotidian Immigration Officers somehow managed to exist on the same stage as the Tibetan dancers and, unknowingly, played out a Buddhist parable at the same time. Nice one Paul…

After *World's Apart* we decided to go even further out on our theatrical particular limb. I'd begun to get interested in European attitudes towards Islam and Paul had met an Islamic feminist… My old mate Trudie Goodwin from *The Bill* was looking for a piece of theatre to do having previously worked with me in a couple of Bogdanov Circus epics, and thus *Crusade* was born. It wasn't an easy delivery…

Firstly, we were a long way in front of the socio/poltical curve at that time. Not many in the West were giving any thought to Islam in the early/mid nineties. But TRSE was in Newham, East London, and our community contacts were telling us that something was definitely going on.

To my undying shame, my eldest brother Tony was a Morris dancer who also performed in a Mummer's play (but only on Boxing Day). He provided us with a semi-traditional script which soon found its way into the play. Our point was that The Crusades still played a part in shaping European attitudes to Islam (and now, apparently, some radical Muslim attitudes to Europe and America). However, when we finally presented the piece we ran into a bit of a storm.

Reviewers tended not to like it, but perhaps more for its content than its dramatic form or presentation. However, we did actually get a few van loads of Muslim youth, especially women, turning up to see it and local response was generally good. Some commentators thought we were stirring-up unnecessary trouble, however, it was reported back to me that the production 'saved our council grant'. See what you think, especially given your present gift of retrospection.

Anyway, Jenny Tiramani came up with a great set and Bob Irwin, our long-suffering production manager at the time, even managed to get the van to drive on stage (most nights).

One typical TRSE memory – Trudie's third line, the van

having stalled somewhere in the Sinai Desert, was 'Where are we?'. On press night she got the resonant answer 'Stratford!' from one local stalwart.

Paul moved on to greater things after *Crusade*, whilst remaining a resident writer at TRSE (he's still doing stuff with them now at the time of writing this in 2008). However, we kept in touch, especially over the play *Skaville*, an early version of which I had commissioned, published in Volume One. *This Other Eden* we did talk about but I only really caught up with when it was done at Essex University. In my previous introduction I talked about Paul's musicality as a writer. *This Other Eden* clearly bears this out, it is, indeed, a 'quartet', a somewhat dissonant one at times but there certainly are four, intertwined voices. The script also gives the actors, and maybe even the director, to 'riff' a little, shove the text about a bit. Paul is a jazzer at heart after all…

International Café I've only just managed to read, and enjoyed very much. And, I can't help feeling that Salvatore's football match header story may well go back to an anecdote I once told Paul about the immortal Frankie Worthington playing for Leicester. Some of it reminds me of conversations I've had in and around Rick Stein's fish place in Padstow. Perhaps we could get the great man himself to do it there? Or, there's a very-mixed menu restaurant in Bangalore that would fit the bill very well… Paul?

I guess, for me, the most important thing is that Paul, always a talented writer, has developed into a bloody good playwright. We did a reading of *Bad Blood Blues* at the Soho Theatre just recently as part of our Theatrescience programme (again featuring Ms Goodwin). People laughed (a lot), cried a bit and were engaged in an important social issue (HIV). Sounds like theatre to me. Hopefully it will appear in 'Sirett Plays Vol 3'.

Jeff Teare
October 2008

For Natalie, Joe and Elena

WORLDS APART

ABBREVIATIONS

CIO	Chief Immigration Officer
IO	Immigration Officer
PA	Political Asylum
TA	Temporary Admission
SEA	Secondary Examination Area
PAQ	Political Asylum Questionnaire
IS81	Immigration Service Form 81 (given to detainees who are to be questioned)
PMI	Port Medical Inspector

THE STORY OF SUKYI NYIMA

This story is taken from a Tibetan Folk Opera. Its purpose in the play is as a narrative for the office politics and personal relationships of the immigration officers.

Characters

CHIEF IMMIGRATION OFFICER DAVE SULLIVAN
a middle-aged career Civil Servant from Yorkshire

IMMIGRATION OFFICER STEVE LUCAS
in his mid-thirties. Welsh

IMMIGRATION OFFICER ROB PARRY
a disaffected Liverpudlian, in his thirties

IMMIGRATION OFFICER ROWENA BARRATT
an ex-policewoman in her thirties from the west country

IMMIGRATION OFFICER SUSAN NEALE
a recent languages graduate in her early twenties. Home
counties / London

IMMIGRATION OFFICER JANET MILLER*
a member of the new shift, seen only at the end of the play

PHURBU TSERING
Narrator. Member of a Chinese-run Tibetan
performance troupe. About thirty

DION STANLEY
a large, powerfully built African-American in his mid-twenties.
In the US Air Force, stationed in Germany

MANGBETU
a Zairean woman in her twenties

LEONELLA DE CORVERA
a young Spanish dancer, about twenty

K S RAMALINGHAM
an Asian businessman from the West Midlands,
in his late-thirties

Four lords of the cemeteries can be doubled

* Note: This part can de doubled or played by
an acting member of stage management

Worlds Apart was first performed at the Theatre Royal Stratford East on 28th January 1993 with the following cast:

SULLIVAN,   David Barrass
LUCAS,   Patrick Brennan
PARRY,   Jonathan Coote
BARRATT,   Claire Rushbrook
NEALE,   Hannah Jacobs
MILLER,   Angie Wallis
DION STANLEY,   David Harewood
LEONELLA DECONVERA,   Anya Phillips
PHURBU TSERING,   Richard Rees
MANGBETU,   Joy Richardson
K.S. RAMALINGHAM,   Madhav Sharma

Director,   Jeff Teare
Assistant Director,   Indhu Rubasingham
Designer,   Sue Mayes
Lighting,   Jon Linstrum
Choreography,   Denzil

Act One

Immigration control at a major London airport. Early 1993.

The stage is split into three levels:

1. BOTTOM LEVEL. Immigration office (a typical open plan office) and Immigration officers' rest room (a small, functional room with low chairs, a sink, fridge, tea/coffee making facilities).

2. MIDDLE LEVEL. The Secondary Examination Area, or SEA, (a waiting area where individuals not allowed through immigration are detained) and an 'open' interview area (a separate, glass partitioned cubicle where detainees are interviewed).

3. TOP LEVEL. A performance area for dancers.

The design should be based on a Tibetan temple, with the levels representing devils at the bottom, mortals in the middle, and spirits at the top.

The SEA is the only part of the set that is occupied at the start of the play. DION STANLEY is asleep; MANGBETU is sitting as far away from DION as possible, staring into the middle distance. The lights come up on four masked skeleton-like figures standing behind a gauze on the top level. These figures are Tibetan lords of the cemeteries. They are standing in front of a brightly coloured tangka.

The sound of an overflying airplane fills the auditorium. At the same time the lords of the cemeteries fade from view and we hear an airport acoustic – tannoy announcements, voices, footsteps; it is mid-afternoon, about 4 pm. PARRY enters the SEA from the arrivals floor with PHURBU TSERING.

PARRY: Wait here.
> *(PARRY enters the office and makes a phone call. LUCAS enters the office, he collects a file and then exits. PARRY concludes his phone call, then exits.*
> *PHURBU looks around the SEA, and grinning, turns to face the audience.)*
PHURBU: (*To audience.*) As the plane landed I was reminded of a humorous story… The story has it that ex-President

Reagan, the disgraced East German leader Erich Honecker, and the retired Chinese communist Deng Xiaoping, finding themselves together on the same flight began to boast about the loyalty of their bodyguards. Reagan said to his bodyguard, 'You must prove that you are the most loyal by jumping from this plane without a parachute'. 'But, Mr Reagan,' pleaded the bodyguard, 'I have a wife and family back home, please don't make me jump.' And so Reagan gave in and said he did not have to do it. Then Honecker said to his bodyguard, 'You must prove that you are the most loyal by jumping from this plane without a parachute'. 'But I have a wife and family back home,' cried the unhappy bodyguard. 'Very well, you do not have to jump,' said Honecker. Then Deng Xiaoping called his bodyguard over and whispered something in his ear. Immediately the bodyguard threw open the plane door and plunged to his death. 'That's incredible,' said Reagan. 'What did you say to him?' 'Nothing much,' replied Deng. 'I simply reminded him that back home he has a wife and family.'

(*DION wakes up.*)

But this isn't the story I want to tell you. I want to tell you a parable, the story of Sukyi Nyima. This story would usually be spoken as the narrative of an opera – we are going to present it in a slightly different and adapted form tonight. At the same time you will also see an account of my detention at this airport. The story of Sukyi Nyima begins with an old couple who, after seeking teachings from the hermit saint, Dhangsong, present him with a white loincloth as a gift. That night Dhangsong experiences a wet dream –

DION: An opera about a wet dream!

PHURBU: This is Dion, an American serviceman, stationed in Germany.

DION: Bet you wouldn't get Pavarotti singing that.

PHURBU: Like myself, Dion has been detained by immigration here at the airport. (*Indicating MANGBETU.*) And Mangbetu, from Kinshasa, Zaire. Her husband is here in Britain – She hopes to join him. To continue… the following morning Dhangsong washes the garment in a stream. While he does so a female deer comes to drink the water and as a consequence, seems to be affected by something unusual. Dhangsong takes special care of her, and nine months later amid extraordinary rainbows and uncommonly bright sunshine the deer gives birth to a human girl –

DION: You expect us to believe that!

PHURBU: It is called symbology.

DION: It's called bestiality, pal.

(*DION goes back to sleep.*)

PHURBU: Dhangsong names the child Sukyi Nyima, meaning 'Sun's Body'.

(*SUSAN NEALE enters the office. There is no one in the office so NEALE exits.*)

Meanwhile in the same Kingdom, there was a Queen who desperately wanted children so she performed special pujas – prayers – for fertility and gave birth to a son, Dawe Senga, meaning 'Moon's Lion'.

(*SULLIVAN enters the office and busies himself sorting through some files on his desk.*)

The Queen again becomes pregnant and gives birth to a second son – he's not in this version – And so the years pass and the day comes when the King must choose which son should succeed him...

(*PARRY enters the office.*)

PARRY: Did you get the Pope's blessing?

SULLIVAN: Don't start, Parry. I'm not in the mood.

PARRY: What? I only asked how you got on.

SULLIVAN: Well, don't. Where's that Zairean woman's passport?

PARRY: Barratt took it. Said you wanted someone to have a look at the visa.

SULLIVAN: When did she go?

PARRY: Twenty minutes? I don't know... She was still here when I left. I had to go down to gate twenty-seven.

SULLIVAN: Anything I should know about?

PARRY: A flight from Luanda.

SULLIVAN: Since when did we start taking flights direct from Angola?

PARRY: It was some kind of cargo flight. They're due to fly back out again tonight. The surveillance team pulled someone out of the hold. No documents, no passport, nothing.

(*PHURBU points to himself.*)

He's already claiming political asylum.

(*LUCAS enters the office.*)

SULLIVAN: That doesn't exactly surprise me.

PARRY: He's Chinese. At least, I think he is. Well, sort of south Asian-Chinese. He's not African, put it that way.

SULLIVAN: African-Asian?

PARRY: Don't think so. Besides there's none of them left out there now, they all came over here in the '70s.

SULLIVAN: What was he doing in Angola?

PARRY: No idea… He kept grinning at me. Every time I looked at him, this inane grin spread over his face like I was doing him some big favour.

SULLIVAN: Have you notified the charter company?

PARRY: Not yet.

SULLIVAN: Well, what are you waiting for?

(*SULLIVAN hands the phone to PARRY. PARRY starts to punch in a number.*)

Can he speak any English?

PARRY: Yes.

(*SULLIVAN takes the phone and replaces the receiver. BARRATT enters the office.*)

SULLIVAN: Interview him first. He can't do a runner in one country and then just turn up here. Find out what he was doing in Luanda.

PARRY: He's probably already claimed asylum out there.

SULLIVAN: In Angola?

PARRY: Well, I don't know do I.

SULLIVAN: I'll tell you one thing; we start getting regular flights from Angola we'll have hundreds a day coming through. Best thing we can do is put a stop to it here and now. Might be able to get him back out tonight if we can get Home Office approval early enough.

BARRATT: How was the board?

SULLIVAN: Christ knows… It's either me or Taylor. The Director of Ports was being a right bastard. Tried to get me to do a complete character assassination on Taylor, but I wasn't having it.

PARRY: What a wasted opportunity.

SULLIVAN: When I want your opinion, Parry, I'll ask for it.

BARRATT: The visa on that Zairean passport is forged.

SULLIVAN: Alright, I'll leave it with you. By the way, no details as yet, but we've got a new one joining the team this afternoon. So no pissing about. And that means you, Parry. I don't want you getting up to none of your stupid games. Clear?

PARRY: As if I would.

SULLIVAN: Steve, sort out that American will you. Go down to customs and see if you can get someone to do a bag search for us. There might be drugs involved.

LUCAS: What if no one's available?

PARRY: (*Imitating LUCAS's Welsh accent.*) You'll have to do it yourself then, won't you. Anyway, I thought you liked rummaging around in other bloke's underpants.

SULLIVAN: Shut up, Parry. (*To LUCAS.*) Just go and get someone.

(*LUCAS turns to go.*)

PARRY: Careful though, you never know what you might find crawling up your shirt sleeves… Do you remember that Nigerian who had those giant snails in his luggage?

SULLIVAN: Shut up, Parry. (*To LUCAS.*) Go on.

(*LUCAS exits. Phone rings.*)

(*To PARRY.*) And you can wipe that smile off your face. Get in there and interview that PA.

(*SULLIVAN answers the phone. PARRY pulls open a drawer to find a questionnaire.*)

(*On phone.*) Yes… Yes… On my way. (*Hangs up – to BARRATT.*) There's some kind of argument going on out on the floor. I'll be back in a minute.

(*SULLIVAN exits.*)

PARRY: You should be ashamed of yourself.

BARRATT: What are you talking about?

PARRY: You and Sullivan. Don't look so surprised. It's common knowledge.

BARRATT: You've got a sordid imagination.

PARRY: Me? You're the one with the sordid imagination. It's you that sleeps with him. He won't want to know you if he gets this promotion.

BARRATT: Is that right?

PARRY: I don't know what it is you see in him, anyway. It can't be his money or his good looks. Perhaps it's his bad breath? Perhaps it's his warm, Yorkshire sense of humour? Perhaps it's the way he dresses? The action slacks and bri–nylon shirts… A man whose greatest passions are Yorkshire county cricket club and Crufts.

BARRATT: Crawl back under your stone, Parry.

PARRY: He was an adventure scout, you know. Boys will be boys… You better keep an eye on him and Steve Lucas.

BARRATT: I worry about you sometimes.

(*BARRATT exits. SULLIVAN and K S RAMALINGHAM can be heard ouside the SEA, their voices raised in argument.*)

PHURBU: (*To audience, as arguement outside continues.*) My companions and I had been detained in a room referred to by the immigration officers as the SEA, the Secondary Examination Area. After a while we were joined by Mr K S Ramalingham, voted young entrepreneur of the year in 1980 by the Chamber of Commerce in Wolverhampton, he is now a successful businessman living in Birmingham. He has mislaid his passport.

(*SULLIVAN and K S RAMALINGHAM enter the SEA.*)

K S: This is ridiculous. What is your name? I demand to know your name. What is your name?

SULLIVAN: Mr Ramalingham, I cannot allow you to simply waltz through immigration without a passport.

K S: I told you, I left it in the departure lounge at Charles de Gaulle.

SULLIVAN: You often leave your passport behind, do you, sir?

K S: I was looking for something in my suitcase… I was in a rush, the plane was boarding I must've left it on the seat.

SULLIVAN: I don't care if you tore it up and used it for confetti. You're not going through until we check your details.

K S: (*Furious.*) This is an outrage!

SULLIVAN: Why don't you calm down, then perhaps we might be able to have a sensible conversation about this.

K S: I am perfectly calm. You want proof of who I am, I'll give you proof.

(*BARRATT enters the SEA, she crosses to SULLIVAN. K S opens his briefcase, he takes out a Psion organiser and types a request into it. He then takes a mobile phone from his case and hands it to SULLIVAN along with the Psion organiser. PARRY leaves the office and enters the SEA.*)

That is the phone number of my office. Ring them now, they will vouch for me.

SULLIVAN: We'll keep these if you don't mind.

(*SULLIVAN hands the phone and the Psion organiser to BARRATT.*)

K S: What!

SULLIVAN: And we'll make our own enquiries thank you, Mr Ramalingham.

K S: Why? Why? What is this? You won't even let me help you!

SULLIVAN: I'll get someone to ring the number you've given me in due course, but you must understand that even if they confirm what you say, it's still no proof that you're a British Citizen.

(*K S takes out his wallet.*)

K S: Here are credit cards… Here is my membership of Warwickshire County Cricket Club.

SULLIVAN: (*Incredulously.*) Warwickshire…

(*SULLIVAN looks at the membership card.*)

K S: Do you know anything about cricket?

SULLIVAN: Do I know anything about cricket… Do I know anything… I've opened the bowling for West Riding Schools. Freddy Truman once complimented me on my inswinging yorker, said there weren't many kids my age could get it right up there in the block hole.

K S: I saw Truman bowl against India at Edgbaston –

SULLIVAN: (*Disbelieving.*) Really…

K S: Of course young Gavaskar hit him all over the park that day. You know, I think it was tragic that Gower wasn't included in the squad for India this winter. A good series though… (*Improvise, according to score in current/recent test match.*) Played in the true spirit of the game, not like against those bloody Pakistani cheats.

SULLIVAN: That's enough.

K S: What?

SULLIVAN: This proves nothing.

K S: But… Alright… Here. Look. Here is my driving licence. Surely that's enough…

(*SULLIVAN takes the driving licence.*)

SULLIVAN: You told us you lived in Birmingham.

K S: Yes. Yes. Small Heath.

SULLIVAN: This licence gives your address as Wolverhampton.

K S: I've moved… I haven't informed DVLC yet. Why won't you believe me?

SULLIVAN: How are we to know these things aren't forged, or stolen.

K S: They are mine!

(*SULLIVAN hands the licence to BARRATT.*)

SULLIVAN: This officer will be dealing with your case.

K S: You will be very, very, very sorry you have behaved in this way when I get out of here.

DION: Shut the fuck up! (*He sits up.*) What is it with you, you gotta shout all the time? Man's tryin' to get some sleep here.

(*LUCAS enters carrying DION's suitcase.*)

DION: What you doin' with my bag, man?

K S: You have not heard the last of this!

SULLIVAN: Mr Ramalingham, sit down.

LUCAS: (*To SULLIVAN.*) Nobody was available at customs. Do you want me to go through it?

DION: Gimme my bag.

SULLIVAN: Bring it over here, Steve.

DION: No, you bring it over here, 'Steve'.

K S: I have never been treated like this.

(*LUCAS lays the bag on a vacant seat. He leans over the case as if he is listening to it.*)

SULLIVAN: Listen, one more word out of either of you two and I'll make sure you both spend the rest of the week sitting in here.

K S: Did you hear that? Did you hear that!? I have witnesses, I have witnesses you said that. (*To PHURBU.*) You heard what he said…

LUCAS: There's something buzzing in it.

SULLIVAN: What?

LUCAS: Ssssh. Listen. In the bag. There's something buzzing.

(*The officers, except PARRY who remains in the doorway, gather around the bag and listen. DION crosses to them and attempts to peer over their shoulders. There is a brief silence while they listen.*)

SULLIVAN: What have you got in there that could be making that noise?

DION: I don't know.

K S: Perhaps it's a bomb.

DION: It ain't no bomb. Bombs tick, they don't buzz. You think I wouldn't know if I had a bomb in there.

SULLIVAN: Alright, Lucas. Open it up.

K S: Shouldn't we call the bomb squad?

SULLIVAN: I don't think that'll be neccessary.

K S: We can't be certain it isn't a bomb.

SULLIVAN: Has your baggage been left unattended at any time?

DION: How the hell do I know, this is the first time I seen it in seven hours.

SULLIVAN: Open it, Lucas.

LUCAS: Perhaps we should call security.

SULLIVAN: And make ourselves look like bloody idiots… Open it.

(*LUCAS opens the case very carefully. They all nervously peer inside.*)

LUCAS: It's coming from over there… Beneath those boxer shorts.

SULLIVAN: (*To DION.*) Well?

(*DION shrugs his shoulders – he genuinely doesn't have a clue.*)

SULLIVAN: (*Indicating that LUCAS should continue.*) Lucas…

LUCAS: These clothes are filthy.

DION: I was gonna wash them when I got here.

(*LUCAS hesitates.*)

SULLIVAN: Go on, Lucas.

(*LUCAS takes a deep breath and then cautiously pushes his hand into the case. He locates the object and carefully removes it. it is a battery operated Mutant Ninja Turtle. there is a general sigh of relief.*)

DION: My kid musta put it in there.

(*PARRY presses a panic button, setting off an alarm and making everyone jump with fright.*)

SULLIVAN: (*Shouting.*) Parry! What the hell do you think
you're doing! (*Calms down.*) Jesus…

DION: Though I speak with tongues of man and angels and
have not charity, I have become as a sounding brass, or a
tinkling cymbal.

SULLIVAN: What?

DION: It's from the Bible. Corinthians Thirteen. What are you,
some kind of theological retard?

SULLIVAN: What else has he got in there?

(*LUCAS continues his search.*)

LUCAS: Nothing much.

(*DION wanders over to MANGBETU.*)

DION: You wanna sit over here with me?

MANGBETU: (*Aggressively.*) *Je ne me mettrais jamais procher de
vous, non si vous etiez le dernier des hommes!*

DION: I think she likes me.

SULLIVAN: Sit down.

DION: When am I gettin' out of here?

SULLIVAN: When you are prepared to apologize to this officer
(*He indicates BARRATT.*) for the abusive langage you used
at immigration control. And when you can be bothered to
politely explain the purpose and length of your visit, then,
perhaps, we can begin to discuss your entry.

DION: I'm on vacation, man. I already told the bitch. How
many more times!

SULLIVAN: (*To LUCAS.*) Anything?

LUCAS: No. Except…

(*LUCAS holds up a large sealed envelope. He sniffs it, then
shakes it.*)

SULLIVAN: Open it.

(*LUCAS tears open the envelope and peers inside. SULLIVAN takes
the envelope and tips out a handful of flower bulbs.*)

What do we have here then?

DION: They're tulip bulbs. My brother runs a Garden Centre
in Delaware. I went to Amsterdam to get 'em, special.
Listen, I'm in the air force, stationed in Wiesbaden. I
wanted to stop off in Britain for a couple of days to see
some brothers I know before flying on to the States. I'm on
leave, man… You can't get bulbs this quality in the States.

SULLIVAN: What do you take me for?

DION: They're tulip bulbs. Red tulips. Spring-blooming. Long, broad, pointed leaves and single, bell-shaped flowers.

LUCAS: They do look like flower bulbs, Dave.

SULLIVAN: (*To LUCAS.*) Lucas, take his suitcase back and get these looked at…

(*LUCAS closes the case. SULLIVAN and BARRATT exit.*
LUCAS turns to exit.)

DION: Where you goin' with my case, man… Hey…

(*LUCAS exits.*)

Shit.

PARRY: (*To PHURBU.*) This way.

(*PARRY leads PHURBU into the interview area.*)

Sit down. Name, please?

PHURBU: Tsering, Phurbu Tsering.

PARRY: Where were you born, Mr Tsering?

PHURBU: In Kongpo, Southern Tibet. My family now live in Lhasa.

PARRY: What you were doing in Angola?

PHURBU: I am a narrator in a Tibetan Opera and Dance Ensemble. The troupe is on tour in Africa. It is part of a cultural exchange between African countries and the Peoples' Republic of China.

PARRY: Did you request political asylum while you were in Angola?

PHURBU: No.

PARRY: Why have you requested asylum in this country?

PHURBU: I have a cousin here. I met him when the troupe came to Britain five years ago.

PARRY: You've been here before?

PHURBU: Yes.

PARRY: But you didn't want to stay then?

PHURBU: No.

PARRY: Would you mind telling me what happened to make you change your mind?

PHURBU: My brother was arrested after a pro-independence demonstration in Lhasa in 1989. Before, I did not take much interest in politics.

PARRY: Your brother's arrest in some way changed your attitude?

PHURBU: Yes. They took him to Gusta prison. For twelve days he was kept in a kind of rectangular, concrete ditch about six feet by two feet, usually covered by an iron grid. It was about seven feet deep. There was no place to sit, so he had to stand all the time. They gave him only one meal of trin momo a day and black tea.

PARRY: Are you allowed to practise your religion?

PHURBU: Some religious activities are tolerated, but what they call superstitious practices are often condemned or banned.

PARRY: Such as?

PHURBU: Burning incense. Throwing tsampa, barley flour, into the air during ceremonies. Sometimes, even chanting.

PARRY: Have any of these restrictions ever affected you directly?

PHURBU: No.

PARRY: You had no documents when you arrived here.

PHURBU: I couldn't get them. The tour manager keeps all documents. We were due to fly back to China... When I found out about the flight to London... I had to make a choice.

PARRY: You didn't destroy your documents?

PHURBU: No. To me the documents are irrelevant, they are Chinese. I am not Chinese.

(*PARRY hands PHURBU a form.*)

PARRY: I want you to fill in this questionnaire, it's just a few details we need to know.

(*PHURBU stares at the form, then turns to the audience.*)

PHURBU: (*To audience.*) Perhaps I should have stayed with the troupe... But I felt like a foreigner in my own country. Now I was a foreigner in your country... (*He holds up the form.*) There's no point you watching me fill this in...
(*Lights fade on the airport. One masked lord of the cemeteries appears on the top level in front of the tangka. The tangka and figure fade, it is one hour later. PHURBU, DION, K S and MANGBETU sit quietly in the SEA, the only sound is the constant beat coming from the headphones of DION's personal stereo.*)

PHURBU: (*To audience.*) One hour later, we were all still there and beginning to get to know each other.

K S: (*To DION.*) Turn it down, please. Going 'Ka' 'Ka' 'Ka' in my ear all the time. You'll drive me insane.

DION: What?

K S: Turn it off.

(*DION takes off the headphones.*)

DION: What?

K S: Turn this off, please.

(*DION puts the headphones back on. He immediately takes them off again, leaving the cassette playing. PARRY exits from the office.*)

DION: What's your problem, anyway?

K S: I haven't got a problem.

DION: Why don't you shut up, then?

K S: It's you who has the problem.

DION: Me?

K S: Yes, you.

DION: Where you from?

K S: Wolverhampton.

DION: I hate people from Wolverhampton.

K S: You've never been there.

DION: I don't got to go somewhere to hate the people who come from there.

K S: Are you going to turn this rubbish off?

DION: Rubbish! This is the Hammer. Hammer is music.

K S: I don't even know how you have the nerve to call it music. Turn it off.

DION: You name me one musician who's better than Hammer, then I'll turn it off.

K S: Phil Collins.

DION: What!

K S: Elton John.

DION: Shit!

K S: Dire Straits. How many more do you want?

DION: You don't know what you're talkin' about. (*To PHURBU.*) Hey, you. You like Hammer?

PHURBU: (*To audience – mouthing the word.*) Who?

DION: Hey, I'm talkin' to you… Yes, you. You think Hammer is better than Phil Collins?

PHURBU: Does it matter?

DION: So you don't like Hammer?

PHURBU: I've never heard him.

DION: Never heard him!

K S: You haven't missed anything. Besides, you can hear him now with all the rest of us, whether you want to or not.
(*DION crosses to PHURBU with his personal stereo. He hands the headphones to PHURBU.*)

DION: Put 'em on. You're gonna be born again…
(*PHURBU puts the headphones on.*)
You like it?

PHURBU: (*Unable to hear.*) What?

DION: You… (*He removes the headphones.*) You like it?

PHURBU: I…

DION: He's into it. (*To K S.*) You lose, pecker-head. The music stays on for the rest of your life.
(*DION pushes the headphones against K S's ear. K S pushes the headphones away.*)

K S: Did it ever occur to you that if perhaps you listened to proper music it might improve your intellect; help your mind to grow instead of making it numb. If you listen to Dire Straits instead of that terrible American music –

DION: Dire Straits are American.

K S: (*Indignant.*) No they are not!

DION: You're out of control… I'm hungry.
(*DION puts his headphones on again. There is a brief pause.*)

K S: How can I be expected to run a company when they keep me shut in here for no reason. (*He looks at his watch.*) This is very serious. I will write to the Prime Minister. I stood for the council in the last election, you know. We should never have got rid of Margaret Thatcher, this would never have happened under Thatcher. She respected the business community. Even those peasants at the airport in Delhi work faster than these people.

PHURBU: I wanted to go to India.

K S: (*Uninterested.*) Really.

PHURBU: Dharamsala.

K S: So why didn't you?

PHURBU: There was no way to get there from where I was in Africa.
(*DION takes his headphones off.*)

K S: You're better off here. In Great Britain.

DION: What's that?

K S: I wasn't talking to you.

DION: I don't know why you want to live in this corpse of a country in the first place?

K S: How can you say that? You – from the United States of America. We have a special relationship.

DION: Not with me you don't.

K S: America needs Britain.

DION: America runs Britain. That's probably why we're all still waitin' here – they haven't had the fax from the White House tellin' 'em what to do with us yet.

K S: Nonsense.

DION: (*To PHURBU.*) He been sayin' things to you about me?

PHURBU: He was talking about his business.

DION: What business?

K S: Computer software.

DION: I didn't know you had computers in the 3rd World yet.

K S: Third World!

DION: Yeah. Third World.

K S: At least I'm not a drug addict.

(*DION stands menacingly in front of K S.*)

DION: Say that again.

K S: You heard. I sometimes wonder how Desert Storm wasn't a complete disaster. Soldiers like you, taking drugs and running round like chickens with their heads chopped off. It's a miracle there weren't more friendly fire incidents.

DION: You pissin' me, man? I oughta take your head clean off… Clean off…

(*The telephone in the office rings. SULLIVAN enters. He answers the phone and holds a brief conversation.*)

PHURBU: (*To the audience.*) It's about time we got back to the story of Sukyi Nyima. After confering with his ministers as to which son should succeed him, the King decides upon Dawe Senga. However, before the coronation can take place, it is necessary for the Prince to visit the temple of his Father's God and perform a puja there.

(*LUCAS enters the office. SULLIVAN finishes the phone conversation.*)

SULLIVAN: Steve, come with me.

(*PARRY enters the office.*)

(*To LUCAS.*) I've got to see the Assistant Director. I'll probably not be around much over the next couple of days so I want you to keep an eye on things for me. I'll brief you on the way… I've got it.

LUCAS: The promotion?

PARRY: Well done.

LUCAS: Well done.

PHURBU: And so Dawe Senge sets off to visit the temple with a wise minister.

(*LUCAS and SULLIVAN turn to leave the office. BARRATT enters, she is carrying a passport and 'the book' (a book containing information about possible terrorists).*)

PHURBU: On the way they encounter a girl with whom Dawe Senga is infatuated.

BARRATT: Dave, that Basque girl the Spanish police asked us to keep an eye open for, well look… (*She indicates a reference in 'the book'.*) I stopped this woman going through the BC channel just now… (*She realises SULLIVAN is staring at her without having looked at 'the book'.*) What?… You got it! I'm so pleased for you.

PHURBU: However, the wise minister seems to distrust the girl.

LUCAS: Watch out, she'll be after your job now.

SULLIVAN: Pull her in – the Spanish girl. I'll alert security.

BARRATT: Do you want me to see what I can get out of her?

SULLIVAN: No. Not yet. Let her sweat for a bit. Make her wonder what we're up to. Parry, get that PA photographed.

(*PARRY exits.*)

(*To BARRATT.*) We can run her details through the computer when I get back.

(*LUCAS and SULLIVAN exit. PARRY enters the SEA.*)

PARRY: Mr Tsering…

K S: Do you know if my details have been confirmed yet?

PARRY: No… Mr Tsering

PHURBU: (*To audience.*) Excuse me.

(*Before exiting PHURBU turns back to the audience. PARRY is waylaid by DION.*)

(*To audience.*) While I'm away the other detainees will be joined by Leonella de Corvera, a young dancer from Spain – the terrorist suspect. She has something to hide.

K S: My details –

(*PARRY ignores K S and exits with PHURBU. BARRATT enters the SEA.*)

You. Yes, you…

MANGBETU: Please…

> (*BARRATT ignores K S and MANGBETU and walks straight through the SEA.*)

K S: Please will you tell me –

> (*BARRATT exits.*)

I hope they realise that I shall be claiming compensation from the Home Office for the time they have wasted today. I am a very important man. Two hours I've been sitting here. It's not good enough –

> (*The door opens. K S jumps back, he is momentarily silenced. BARRATT re-enters the SEA with LEONELLA DE CORVERA.*)

BARRATT: (*To LEONELLA – as she enters.*) We won't keep you long. The chief immigration officer just wanted me to check a few details.

LEONELLA: What's the problem?

BARRATT: I'm sure it's nothing serious.

K S: Will you kindly tell me how much longer you intend to keep me waiting here?

BARRATT: Can't you see I'm dealing with someone else.

K S: I will not stand for this incompetence.

BARRATT: It was you who arrived here without a passport, Mr Ramalingham. That's hardly my fault, is it?

LEONELLA: I have to be (*She hands BARRATT a handbill.*) here…at half past six. It is very important.

BARRATT: There's plenty of time yet. Just sit down there.

K S: I am a member of the National Trust. I have shares in British Telecom. I have had an article on my company in the *Mail on Sunday*. I am not an immigrant. I am not a refugee. I am not an alien!

> (*PHURBU and PARRY enter the SEA. BARRATT glances at them then exits. PARRY leaves PHURBU and exits. BARRATT enters the office, passing through it to the rest room. During PHURBU's following speech BARRATT takes a bottle of champagne from the fridge and places the champagne and some glasses on a tray. PARRY enters the rest room as she takes the tray into the office. He follows her in.*)

PHURBU: After being chosen to succeed the King and praying to his Father's God, Dawe Senge asks of an oracle where he might obtain a suitable wife. He is told that she will be found in the South, and since that was where Dawe Senge and his minister met the girl, he assumes that she must be destined for his bride. While travelling home, Dawe Senge is again waylaid by the girl with offers of chang, that is beer, he is seduced and makes Rigngen Bhumo his Queen. (*SULLIVAN and LUCAS enter the office. BARRATT is waiting with the champagne.*)

SULLIVAN: What's this?

BARRATT: I thought we might celebrate your promotion.

(*BARRATT hands SULLIVAN the champagne.*)

SULLIVAN: (*To BARRATT.*) What if I hadn't got it?

BARRATT: There was never any doubt.

(*BARRATT leans over and kisses SULLIVAN.*)

SULLIVAN: (*Slightly embarrassed.*) I suppose I might as well put you people in the picture – As I am shortly to be promoted to Inspector and won't be directly associated with you two any more – I O Rowena Barratt and I are... Well, we've been seeing each other.

PARRY: As if we didn't know.

LUCAS: I didn't.

BARRATT: And we're going to be getting engaged.

LUCAS: Well, congratulations, I suppose.

PHURBU: The special advisor to the King, a patriotic parrot –

DION: A what!... Hey, no problem. A patriotic parrot is cool.

PHURBU: A patriotic parrot questions Dawe Senge about his wife's background, but Dawe Senge is too much in love with her to care.

LUCAS: Dave, are you sure about this? I mean, she is an ex-policewoman, you know.

SULLIVAN: Leave it out, you. I know what I'm doing. (*He raises his glass.*) Cheers.

ALL: Cheers.

(*In the SEA MANGBETU starts rocking back and forth on her seat as if she is going to be sick. LEONELLA crosses to her. PARRY leaves the office and crosses into the rest room.*)

PHURBU: One day a hunter falls asleep in the palace grounds. When he wakes up he finds an extraordinarily beautiful girl, Sukyi Nyima, standing beside him. In her hand she holds a rosary of a hundred and eight pearls given to her by the hermit saint Dhangsong which has the power to protect her.

(*NEALE enters the rest room. She is holding a necklace.*)

NEALE: Excuse me… (*She sees PARRY staring at the necklace.*) Oh, the clasp's broken. Do you know where I might find Chief Immigration Officer Sullivan?

PARRY: Wait here, I'll get him.

PHURBU: Anticipating a rich reward the hunter goes to tell King Dawe Senge about his discovery.

(*PARRY crosses into the office and whispers into SULLIVAN's ear.*)

The King upon hearing about Sukyi Nyima sets off with the hunter to investigate.

(*PARRY and SULLIVAN cross into the rest room.*)

NEALE: (*Offering her hand to SULLIVAN.*) Susan Neale… Your new I O.

SULLIVAN: Dave Sullivan. It's great to have you on the team. Come and meet the others.

(*SULLIVAN, NEALE and PARRY cross into the office.*)

Excuse all the booze. It's not normally like this, I've just been promoted to Inspector.

NEALE: Congratulations.

SULLIVAN: Susan, this is Steve. Parry you've met. And this is Rowena.

BARRATT: Have a glass of champagne.

NEALE: Thank you.

(*LEONELLA bangs on the door that leads into the office.*)

LEONELLA: (*Calling from the SEA.*) Please…

SULLIVAN: See what's happening, Steve.

(*LUCAS exits.*)

PHURBU: Enough of our parable for now, we must concentrate on the story of the detainees.

(*LUCAS enters the SEA and crosses to MANGBETU with LEONELLA.*)

SULLIVAN: (*To NEALE.*) Anything wrong? Not shy, are you?… You'll be alright. You'll make the grade. You'd have to be bloody awful not to. Get through the next six months and you can do what you bloody like. Once the new Bill's gone through things'll be a lot more straightforward.

PARRY: If you like spending all day fingerprinting people.

(*LUCAS leaves the SEA and immediately re-enters the office.*)

LUCAS: Dave, it's the Zairean woman. I think she's sick.

SULLIVAN: Rowena. Get in there, will you.

BARRATT: Do you think she's a mule?

SULLIVAN: Maybe. (*To NEALE.*) Had a woman here last week,
48 condoms of pure cocaine she had in her. Bloody death
wish. (*To BARRATT.*) You going?

(*BARRATT and LUCAS leave the office and enter the SEA.*)

(*To NEALE.*) Forged visa, this one. You'll have to watch out
for forgeries. The Zaireans are getting better all the time.
So be on your guard. Mind, they've a long way to go to
before they're as good as the Pakistanis. The Bengalis are
bloody useless, shouldn't have any trouble with them.
Shall I tell you what makes the best Immigration Officers?
Common sense. Simple, bloody common sense. If you're
suspicious of someone, use your common sense. We want
to get people off the premises a.s.a.p., unless it's in our best
interests to keep them here where we can keep an eye on
them, of course. Common sense, that's what it all comes
down to, we're not looking for academic geniuses straight
out of university, we've got plenty of them, and most of
them are bloody useless…

(*LUCAS leaves the SEA and re-enters the office. BARRATT
follows him.*)

LUCAS: (*To SULLIVAN.*) We're going to have to get her to the
PMI.

BARRATT: She's fine – She's pregnant, that's all.

LUCAS: She needs to see a doctor.

BARRATT: She doesn't need a doctor. It's just nausea. I can't
believe she thought she'd get away with it. We were bound
to find out sooner or later.

SULLIVAN: Are you positive?

BARRATT: I felt it kick.

LUCAS: Dave…

(*LUCAS takes SULLIVAN to one side.*)

We have to notify the PMI – What if something happens
while she's in our custody? We can't take chances.

SULLIVAN: Rowena knows what she's doing.

LUCAS: You can't just leave her in there. We are supposed to
record the fact that she's ill.

SULLIVAN: Don't you tell me my job. (*To NEALE.*) Can you speak French?

NEALE: I read French at university.

SULLIVAN: …Right. Well, that'll save us having to mess around with a bloody interpreter then, won't it. Rowena, brief Susan on the Zairean. (*To NEALE.*) She does speak some English, but it'll be useful to have you on it… (*To the others.*) Come on, Ladies and Gents, your glasses please. There's work to be done.

(*SULLIVAN sits at his computer and begins to type. LUCAS goes to a desk and gets on with some paper work – he stops what he is doing in order to listen to the following conversation between SULLIVAN and PARRY.*)

(*To PARRY – as he types.*) Have you sorted out that Chinese asylum case you were dealing with?

PARRY: The Home Office have got all the details. I don't think there'll be a problem. He's been photographed.

SULLIVAN: Am I right in thinking the charter company still haven't been contacted?

PARRY: Yes.

SULLIVAN: Good. Go down, find one of the crew and tell them they're taking a passenger out with them tonight. Warn them we might have to delay their return flight. If they get difficult remind them that someone came in on their flight this afternoon without proper documentation and if they don't co-operate it won't just be the two thousand pound fine, they'll get their license suspended and all. (*Holding out tray with the bottle and glasses on.*) Do something with these will you…

(*PARRY takes the tray into the rest room, then exits.*)

(*To BARRATT.*) Rowena, you better notify the police about that Spanish girl, there's nothing on our computer. We'll have to wait for them to advise us.

(*BARRATT returns some forms to the cabinet. SULLIVAN crosses to NEALE. In the SEA, LEONELLA is pacing the floor.*)

I remember 1968. When I first started. I had to interview a young Czech. He'd come all the way from Prague in the undercarriage of a plane. He was blue when they found him. I took him to the bar and poured brandies down his throat, which I later found out was precisely the wrong thing to do… It's a tough job, you soon find that out, but it's worth doing. In one sense, you know, we are the thin blue line. After us, Armageddon…

(*SULLIVAN takes a toffee from his pocket and puts it in his mouth.*)

Toffee?

(*SULLIVAN offers a toffee to NEALE. NEALE takes one, as she does so SULLIVAN places his hand on hers.*)

Don't tell no one, or they'll all want one. (*He lays a hand on her shoulder.*) You'll fit in just fine.

(*SULLIVAN turns to see BARRATT staring at him.*)

You can interview the Zairean when you get back.

(*BARRATT exits. In the SEA LEONELLA continues to pace the floor.*)

LEONELLA: Did they ever come to Spain?

K S: No. They were on *Opportunity Knocks* once though. Came second. They'd've won if it hadn't been for that bloody Lena Zavaroni…

LEONELLA: What sort of thing did they do?

K S: All sorts. Used to do all their own choreography you know. Oh yes. As good as any dance group in London. They did all the hits, 'Hot Love' by T Rex, used to have these fantastic cowboy outfits for that. What else? 'Jean Genie' by David Bowie, in Space costumes. Slade – they were from Wolverhampton –

DION: (*To LEONELLA.*) Do it… Hey, you dance for me, I'll dance for you.

(*LEONELLA does a brief, aggressive flamenco dance. At the end of it everyone in the SEA applauds.*)

My turn.

(*DION jumps up, he grabs MANGBETU.*)

MANGBETU: Non, non…

(*DION dances around MANGBETU in an exaggeratedly sexual way. LEONELLA claps along. K S, PHURBU, and even MANGBETU, laugh at the spectacle. The dance builds to a peak at which point SULLIVAN enters, silencing them and killing the atmosphere.*)

SULLIVAN: What the hell's going on?

(*SULLIVAN stares at the detainees for a moment. PHURBU begins quietly chanting the mantra 'Om mani padme hum'.*)

SULLIVAN: You can save your tribal dancing for the bloody
Edinburgh Festival. (*To PHURBU.*) And you can shut up!
(*SULLIVAN exits.*)

PHURBU: (*To audience.*) The Chinese often have a similar
reaction…

(*Lights fade on the airport. Two lords of the cemeteries appear
in front of the tangka on the top level. The tangka and lords of
the cemeteries fade from view, it is early evening. DION, K S,
LEONELLA and MANGBETU sit in silence. PHURBU stands.
SULLIVAN is in the rest room. NEALE is sorting through some
notes in the office.*)

(*To audience.*) Early evening… It was about now that things
really started to get complicated.

(*LUCAS enters the rest room.*)

SULLIVAN: Anything on those bulbs of yours yet?

LUCAS: I haven't heard back.

SULLIVAN: You'd better see if he's carrying. Can't take any
chances…

(*LUCAS goes into the office. SULLIVAN follows him, carrying a
cup of coffee. BARRATT enters the office. SULLIVAN hands the
coffee to NEALE.*)

NEALE: Thanks.

(*SULLIVAN puts a mint into his mouth – he offers one to NEALE,
she declines.*)

SULLIVAN: (*To BARRATT.*) All done?

BARRATT: The police'll contact us as soon as they hear
anything…from Spain.

SULLIVAN: Great, I've filled Neale in on all our procedural
details.

BARRATT: (*Under her breath.*) I bet you have.

(*SULLIVAN chooses to ignore her remark.*)

SULLIVAN: You'd better interview the Zairean woman.
Remember, she's got a forged visa, but she doesn't know
we know – yet. Use it. She doesn't know we know she's
pregnant. Use it. One more thing, she hasn't asked for
political asylum, so don't encourage her.

NEALE: How do you know she'll request asylum?

SULLIVAN: Because I've seen her sort before. You can more
often than not identify PAs just by their racial look.

Usually black, poorly dressed, uneducated, no money, no documents… You'll learn.

(*NEALE gets up to go with BARRATT into the sea.*)

Finish your coffee first.

(*In the SEA, LEONELLA leans against the wall with her head in her hands.*)

DION: (*To LEONELLA.*) Hey, c'mon… It ain't so bad. You wanna dance, you dance with me. I got music. You like Hammer?

LEONELLA: Of course.

DION: (*To K S.*) Hey, you hear that? (*To LEONELLA.*) Come on. (*DION goes to pull LEONELLA over to him. She steps away from him.*)

LEONELLA: No… They know. That's why they're keeping me here. It's not my fault… He made me…

DION: Who? Made you what? You murder someone?

LEONELLA: No.

DION: You a dealer?

LEONELLA: No! These, these… (*LEONELLA opens a paperback and pulls out some photographs.*) My partner, he took them in Madrid last year. He said I was to take them to a newspaper he contacted here – they offered money.

DION: So you ain't a dancer?

LEONELLA: I am. He's my dance partner. We're in the competition together. He used the opportunity of coming here and sell the photographs. I had to bring them or he wouldn't dance with me in the competition.

DION: I don't understand.

LEONELLA: Hugo, my partner, he came over early to make a deal – He wasn't sure if the newspaper wanted the photographs, but when he met them yesterday they said yes, so he called me and said I was to bring them. He said there would be no problem.

DION: You always do what he says?

LEONELLA: I didn't want to do it. He's my partner, I can't get another one, not just like that… All I ever wanted was to dance, but Hugo… I realised too late he doesn't care any more. He's more interested in making deals, taking his photos and becoming paparazzi. I hate all this, but I had to do what he said.

DION: Hey, it's not your fault.

LEONELLA: Who's going to explain that to them? You? Don't you see – They must know I have the photos… They've found out about the photos, they've arrested Hugo – Now they're just waiting for me to turn up because he didn't have them with him. And he will have blamed me, sometimes he'll say anything…

DION: Woah! Time out, time out, just calm down.

LEONELLA: (*Angry.*) You know better, do you? Then you tell me why I'm here, you tell me that!

DION: Hey, hold it, hold it… So, what you gonna do?

LEONELLA: I don't know. But I can forget my career as a dancer. They are bound to search me, try to get the photos off me, get information out of me.

DION: Who's in the photographs?

LEONELLA: I don't know – A British politician, Hugo said. They must suspect I have them… Do you think they know…? Will they send me to prison?

(*DION looks at the photos.*)

DION: Hey, this is explicit stuff…

K S: Let me see… Let me see…

DION: Slow down, Trigger.

(*DION shields the photos from K S.*)

K S: Who is it? Gerald Kaufman?

DION: Who?

K S: Let me see!

(*DION shows the photos to K S.*)

K S: Oh my God. It's… It's… I don't believe it.

LEONELLA: You recognise him?

K S: Of course I recognise him!… (*K S hands the photos back to DION.*) What is happening to the Conservative Party… How could he do this… He's completely naked.

DION: All four of 'em are naked. (*To MANGBETU.*) Look.

MANGBETU: *Non, non.*

DION: Come on. Have a look.

K S: No one must ever see these photographs. Give them to me.

(*LUCAS enters the SEA.*)

LUCAS: Mr Stanley.

(*DION hides the photos behind his back.*)

DION: Steve! Hi! How you doin'?

(*DION pushes the photos into MANGBETU's hands. She lays on the photos and pretends to be asleep.*)

Call me Dion.

LUCAS: Will you come with me, please.

DION: Not now, man. I'm busy... Hey, only kiddin'. What's happnin'? You got my tulip bulbs?

LUCAS: No.

(*BARRATT and NEALE enter the SEA and cross to MANGBETU.*)

DION: (*To LUCAS.*) So where we goin'?

LUCAS: I'm afraid, we're going to have to do a body search.

DION: What's the problem, you think I got some geraniums up my ass?

BARRATT: (*To MANGBETU.*) Wake up... Wake up...

DION: Hey, what you doin'?

BARRATT: (*To LUCAS.*) Are you meant to be taking him out, or what?

K S: (*Standing.*) Excuse me, I would also like to go now.

BARRATT: Sit down and shut up. (*Shaking MANGBETU again.*) Wake up.

LUCAS: Come on.

(*DION does not move. MANGBETU stirs.*)

DION: She ain't been feelin' too good.

NEALE: *Vous vous sentez bien?*

MANGBETU: *Je n'ai rien.*

NEALE: She says there's nothing wrong.

BARRATT: She would, wouldn't she. (*To MANGBETU.*) We're going to interview you now. Will you come with us, please.

(*MANGBETU looks at NEALE.*)

NEALE: *Nous voulons vous interroger maintenant.*

(*LUCAS opens the door that leads out of the SEA to the arrivals floor.*)

LUCAS: Let's go.

(*BARRATT leans over as if she is going to lift MANGBETU. DION grabs his sweat-shirt and flicks the sleeve at BARRATT's backside.*)

BARRATT: Don't you dare do that!

DION: Why? What you gonna do? Turn green and bust outta your shirt?

BARRATT: (*To NEALE.*) Are you just going to stand there?

NEALE: What am I meant to do?

BARRATT: Forget it. Steve…

(*BARRATT attempts to lift MANGBETU. DION flicks BARRATT with his sweat-shirt again. She holds out an accusing finger, DION grabs her hand and bites into it.*)

Get off! Get him off!

(*DION keeps his jaw clamped on BARRATT's hand as LUCAS jumps up onto DION's back and rides him round the room. NEALE freezes. BARRATT breaks free and sets off the alarm. DION dumps LUCAS on the floor and attempts to run out through the door that LUCAS has left open, but he has to jump back inside when he sees PARRY coming. DION hides behind the door into the interview area – they don't see him. SULLIVAN enters the SEA from the office. He turns the alarm off.*)

SULLIVAN: What happened?

LUCAS: He bit her.

SULLIVAN: Who did?

LUCAS: The American.

SULLIVAN: Where is he?

LUCAS: I don't know.

(*PARRY quickly looks inside the interview area, but doesn't see DION.*)

SULLIVAN: Well, where's he bloody gone! He can't have vanished into thin air!

PARRY: He might have run out.

SULLIVAN: Eh?

PARRY: The door… (*He points to the door leading to the arrivals floor.*)

SULLIVAN: Who the hell left that open?

PARRY: Don't look at me, it was already open when I got here.

SULLIVAN: You're bloody useless…The lot of you. Steve, alert security. (*To PARRY.*) You, close those doors. Come on Rowena, let's have a look at you.

(*SULLIVAN exits into the office with BARRATT. NEALE and LUCAS exit. PARRY closes the doors and exits. SULLIVAN takes BARRATT into the rest room where he tries to comfort her. In the SEA K S takes the photographs from MANGBETU – no one sees him do this. PARRY enters the rest room.*)

It's alright. You'll live. Let me have a look. Come on…
Hold still.

(*SULLIVAN looks at BARRATT's hand.*)

PARRY: Shall I get the first aid kit?

SULLIVAN: No, He hasn't broken the skin.

(*PARRY leans over and peers at the wound.*)

PARRY: Do you remember that Zambian who bit Frank
Spooner last year? Frank had to go for HIV tests,
everything. He was terrified.

SULLIVAN: Shut up, Parry.

PARRY: It wasn't my fault that maniac bit her. Lucas was the
one in there with her, not me. It was him should've done
something… Spooner got two thousand quid out of the
Criminal Injuries Compensation Board in the end.

SULLIVAN: Parry, do you want a transfer to the Falkland
Islands? Because that's where you'll go if you don't shut
up.

(*NEALE and LUCAS enter the office. PARRY goes into the
office.*)

PARRY: (*To NEALE.*) Don't fancy a weekend in the Malvinas do
you?

(*PARRY exits.*)

NEALE: What's he going on about?

(*LUCAS shrugs. SULLIVAN finishes inspecting the bite mark on
BARRATT's back.*)

BARRATT: It wasn't Steve's fault in there, you know – it was
her. She just stood there.

SULLIVAN: Who?

BARRATT: You know who I'm talking about…You fancy her,
don't you?

SULLIVAN: You're delirious, woman. Here… (*He reaches into his
pocket and takes out some money.*) Go to the bar, get a couple
of drinks in you.

BARRATT: Are you coming?

SULLIVAN: Maybe. I'll have to sort this mess out first.

(*SULLIVAN returns to the office. BARRATT is about to leave
but turns back just before exiting. SULLIVAN puts his hand on
NEALE's hand.*)

Can you manage the Zairean on your own.

NEALE: Yes. I think.

(*BARRATT exits.*)

SULLIVAN: Tell you what – I'll do the interview with you when I've finished tying up a few loose ends here. Should only be a minute.

(*DION launches himself back into the SEA from the interview area, grabbing his American football – which PHURBU has been holding – as he enters.*)

DION: Touch down! Stanley in the end zone…

K S: Mad.

DION: You guys weren't gonna do nothing.

LEONELLA: Are you okay?

DION: Yeah.

LEONELLA: You should't let them see you.

DION: Where am I gonna hide? I can't keep jumpin' behind the door every time someone comes in.

LEONELLA: (*To DION.*) Thank you…for what you did. (*To MANGBETU.*) Merci.

DION: Yeah, well, I got hungry.

(*NEALE enters the SEA – DION is standing adjacent to the office door so that as NEALE enters she does not see him.*)

NEALE: If you'd like to come with me.

(*DION taps NEALE on the shoulder.*)

DION: Hi.

(*NEALE jumps with fright, runs out and immediately re-enters the office.*)

NEALE: He's in there.

SULLIVAN: Who is?

NEALE: Him.

SULLIVAN: How?

LUCAS: Who?

NEALE: Him!

LUCAS: Dion Stanley?

NEALE: Yes.

SULLIVAN: Did he threaten you?

NEALE: No.

SULLIVAN: We can't take chances. Susan, find out where the bloody hell Parry's disappeared to. Steve, you go round the back, I want four security guards outside the SEA in case of trouble. I'll alert the police – We're going to have to get that bastard out of there…

(*Lights fade on airport. The tangka and two lords of the cemeteries appear on the top level. Lights down.*)

(*End of Act One.*)

Act Two

Lights up on tangka and lords of the cemeteries. Then fade from view. As at the end of Act One – a few minutes later. DION, K S, PHURBU, MANGBETU and LEONELLA are in the SEA.

PHURBU: We must now continue with the story of the detainees. A few minutes have elapsed since you were last with us.

(*SULLIVAN enters the office, shortly followed by LUCAS.*)

SULLIVAN: Everything ready?

LUCAS: Four security guards outside. A dog handler and two armed police officers on standby.

SULLIVAN: When we get him out I want you to go with him. Alright?

LUCAS: Do I have any choice?

SULLIVAN: No. Come on.

(*SULLIVAN and LUCAS exit.*)

K S: (*To DION.*) Now what do you propose to do?

DION: Don't worry, I'll think of something.

(*SULLIVAN and LUCAS enter the SEA.*)

SULLIVAN: We'd like you to come with us please, sir.

DION: Sure.

(*DION holds his hands out to LUCAS to be handcuffed.*)

SULLIVAN: That won't be neccessary, sir. As long as you're prepared to behave like a civilized human being we're prepared to treat you like one. (*Indicating that LUCAS should escort DION.*) Steve…

(*LUCAS crosses to DION.*)

DION: (*Holding up his hands.*) Don't shoot, Steve.

(*SULLIVAN opens the door. PARRY enters, he nods to SULLIVAN to indicate that everything is ready for them to come out.*)

SULLIVAN: (*To DION.*) This way… (*Calling out through door.*) Panic over…

(*LUCAS, PARRY and DION exit. NEALE enters from the floor.*)

SULLIVAN: (*To NEALE – pointing to MANGBETU.*) You better take her through. I won't be long.

(*SULLIVAN exits.*)

NEALE: Are you alright?

(*MANGBETU nods.*)

44

You have to be interviewed now… Do you understand?
(*MANGBETU stands. LEONELLA flinches, expecting to see the photographs. NEALE takes MANGBETU through to the interview area.*)

LEONELLA: (*Under her breath.*) Where are they?
(*No one answers her. SULLIVAN re-enters the SEA and crosses to the interview area. LEONELLA buries her head in her hands.*)

SULLIVAN: I'd like you to answer my questions in English.

MANGBETU: I'll try.

SULLIVAN: Right… (*He consults some notes.*) What's the purpose of your visit to Britain?

MANGBETU: To visit friends… *J'ai de la famille ici.*

NEALE: She has family here.

SULLIVAN: Yes… Yes, I can speak French.

NEALE: Sorry.

SULLIVAN: English, please. How long do you intend to stay?

MANGBETU: Three weeks.

SULLIVAN: I don't think you're telling us the truth… Do you know what was making you feel ill?

MANGBETU: I have not been well. *J'ai mal à l'estomac.*

SULLIVAN: What kind of stomach upset?

MANGBETU: *J'ai mal à l'estomac.*

SULLIVAN: English. What kind of stomach upset?

MANGBETU: I don't know.

SULLIVAN: You're pregnant.

MANGBETU: *Non.*

SULLIVAN: We also know that your visa's forged.

MANGBETU: *Non. C'est authentique. Je resterai ici pendent peu de temps. Je vais au mariage d'un ami.*

SULLIVAN: I don't think you're here for a wedding. I think you want to stay here.

MANGBETU: *Non.*

SULLIVAN: Why are you lying?

MANGBETU: Please. I must see my husband.

SULLIVAN: Is he in Britain?

MANGBETU: Yes.

SULLIVAN: Where?

MANGBETU: I don't know. In London… Please, you must help me… My husband… He told me if I say I am pregnant you will not let me in… He talked to some people, they said it would be better to make up a story.

SULLIVAN: What 'people'?

MANGBETU: I don't know. He told me I would have a better chance if I say I just want to visit. The visa cost a great deal of money. *Je veux vivre avec mon mari.*

SULLIVAN: So you admit you want to stay here?

MANGBETU: Yes. My husband cannot go back. A friend, he asked him to look after some things when he went away. My husband said yes. Our shop was searched and it was found that the cases he left were filled with things stolen from an officer in the army. They took my husband, but he escaped and came here. Then he sent for me.

SULLIVAN: Is your husband here, at the airport?

MANGBETU: Perhaps, I don't know.

SULLIVAN: How many months pregnant are you?

MANGBETU: Five months…

SULLIVAN: How long has your husband been here?

MANGBETU: Three months.

SULLIVAN: So it is his?

MANGBETU: Of course. How dare you…

SULLIVAN: Alright, airight. I think that'll do for now.

MANGBETU: What will you do?

SULLIVAN: There are a few details we'll have to sort out. Then you'll be found accomodation for the night.

MANGBETU: I can stay?

SULLIVAN: I'm not at liberty to discuss that right now.

MANGBETU: But there is a chance?

SULLIVAN: You'll be informed in due course.

MANGBETU: My husband said if there is a problem I must ask for political asylum.

SULLIVAN: I don't think so.

MANGBETU: I want political asylum.

SULLIVAN: You can't claim political asylum. You have no grounds.

MANGBETU: Grounds?

NEALE: *Des raisons.*

MANGBETU: My husband is here.

SULLIVAN: Unless you're in immediate danger and can give us conclusive proof of persecution you cannot claim asylum.

MANGBETU: Please, let me see him. I must see him. (*To NEALE.*) Please help me.

(*NEALE looks to SULLIVAN.*)

SULLIVAN: Listen, I'll see what I can do. But no promises. Come on…

(*The telephone in the office rings. PARRY enters and answers it.*)

PARRY: Parry. Yes… Who? Mr Ramalingham.

(*SULLIVAN crosses through the SEA into the office. NEALE escorts MANGBETU into the SEA, then enters the office. PARRY hangs up.*)

SULLIVAN: We've no option but to deny entry.

NEALE: Why?

SULLIVAN: Why? She's presented forged documents, given false information. How many more fraudulent identities is she going to invent for herself once she's in…

(*LUCAS enters the office.*)

(*To LUCAS.*) Well, what's happening with the bloody cannibal?

LUCAS: Don't know yet. We're to go and get him in about five minutes.

SULLIVAN: Right.

(*LUCAS goes to the rest room.*)

SULLIVAN: (*To NEALE.*) Inform customs we're going to need someone to do a search, no rush though. Oh, and you'd better arrange for the PMI to confirm the pregnancy and check her for any dreadful diseases. You can take her over to the detention centre and sort out her deportation later on.

(*SULLIVAN crosses to the rest room, NEALE follows him in.*)

NEALE: So that's it, is it?

SULLIVAN: How do you mean?

NEALE: She requested asylum.

SULLIVAN: Maybe she did. Fact is, Susan, she's not being persecuted. I'm not letting just anyone claim asylum. The only way someone gets to claim it when I'm around is when I know they're for real.

NEALE: And she isn't 'real' enough for you.

SULLIVAN: We can't let her in just because she knows someone else who's here.

NEALE: You mean her husband.

SULLIVAN: We can only guarantee sanctuary to genuine refugees, not economic liabilities.

NEALE: How do you tell the difference?

SULLIVAN: Common sense.

NEALE: You mean, if I don't like the look of someone they don't get in?

SULLIVAN: No, that's not what I mean. What I'm trying to explain is that it's up to us to take the initiative.
(In the office the phone rings again. PARRY takes a message, then crosses to the rest room where he stands staring at SULLIVAN.)

NEALE: Couldn't we grant her temporary admission?

SULLIVAN: She'd do a runner.

NEALE: What about a bail facility?

SULLIVAN: What's she going to use? Beads? She hasn't got anything.

NEALE: But what about her husband? Is she going to see him?

SULLIVAN: No. Susan, there's no point in getting wound up about it. Someone's got to make these decisions. It's not as if it'll get to court. And even if it did that wouldn't affect us. We're only doing what we're paid for. You can't afford to get personally involved.
(SULLIVAN returns to the office. PARRY follows him.)

SULLIVAN: *(To PARRY.)* Do you want something or what?

PARRY: Er, yes... Mr Ramalamadingdong, apparently he is who he says he is.

SULLIVAN: Who?

PARRY: The Asian businessman of the year in there.

SULLIVAN: Oh him... We'll keep him here a bit longer. Might teach him not to leave his passport behind next time.
(In the rest room, LUCAS turns to NEALE.)

LUCAS. Are you alright?

NEALE: She asked me to help her.

LUCAS: It's not your fault.

NEALE: I don't understand why her husband can stay here but she can't.

LUCAS: No...

NEALE: I mean, is there nothing we can do? What possible harm would it be for the woman to see her husband, even if it's only for five minutes... And surely she's within her rights to at least claim asylum. Her husband can't go back. And what's going to happen to her when she arrives back in Zaire? One hell of a welcoming committee, I bet.

LUCAS: Don't concern yourself with it.

NEALE: I wasn't told that it was entirely up to one person to decide who was and who wasn't a genuine asylum seeker.

LUCAS: I do understand.

NEALE: (*Disbelieving.*) Really...

LUCAS: Yes. It's gets to me sometimes. But the vast majority of asylum seekers do get their cases heard.

NEALE: That's hardly any consolation to her, is it.

LUCAS: We have to draw the line somewhere. We don't want drugs dealers, criminals –

NEALE: Does she look like a criminal?

LUCAS: Listen, I mean, I agree they should let her see her husband –

NEALE: Does she have the right of appeal?

LUCAS: No. Even if her case had been officially acknowledged and then officially refused she still wouldn't be able to appeal against it.

NEALE: So, she's powerless.

LUCAS: Did she say if her husband had been waiting for her at the airport?

NEALE: She said it was a possibility.

LUCAS: Then, perhaps there's a chance he could have said something to one of the refugee organisations.

NEALE: What difference would that make?

LUCAS: Sometimes they're able to intervene before...whoever it is, gets sent back. If they can find out that a person is here they can contact a lawyer, and then the lawyer can arrange for the individual to be brought before a court... There's a solicitor, Mark Campbell, he deals with these kind of cases all the time. He's with a client here at the airport today. I saw him on his way over to the police station.

NEALE: I'm not sure you should be telling me this.

LUCAS: I'll shut up then.

NEALE: Have you been here a long time?

LUCAS: Nearly three years. I just kind of drifted into it really, tried a lot of things, I even had a go at teaching, but I hated the kids... They told me there was the opportunity for a lot of travel in the immigration service – Asia, Africa. So I thought, why not... What about you?

NEALE: No idea. Well, that's not strictly true. Shall we just say, there weren't exactly a lot of options. I was getting bits and pieces of translation work, but not enough to live on. I thought I might quite like the job.

LUCAS: And do you?

NEALE: I don't know... If all this is anything to go by...At least it's better than translating French pharmaceutical magazines, I suppose –

(*PARRY enters the rest room.*)

PARRY: What's going on here then? (*To NEALE.*) Not still going on about Miss Zaire 1993, are you?

LUCAS: Don't take no notice of him.

PARRY: (*To LUCAS – with the intention of NEALE overhearing.*) Did I ever tell you about that Ghanaian woman I had to deal with? The one that came here from Portugal? That was a stroke of genius. Fortress Europe, eh – Bollocks to that. They still sneak in through the back door... She was desperate, I had to get her to calm down so I told her we'd decided to let her stay. At this point she's very happy. Anyway, I show her a map and say, 'Well, there's this river here, we have to cross the river and we'll find you some accomodation on the other side.' Then we put her in a van and drove her down to Southampton so we could put her on a ship back to Lisbon. Well, it only seemed right, after all she had come from there in the first place. But somehow she finds out what we were up to. Tries to do a runner and six of us pile into her. We throw her in the back of a police van, her clothes are all ripped and she's hanging out –

NEALE: What are you trying to prove?

PARRY: What?

NEALE: You've had your laugh. Now...just shut up!

PARRY: I was talking to my colleague.

LUCAS: Don't include me in this, Parry.

PARRY: But I thought you were interested. I don't know, whatever happened to the camaraderie, the *esprit de corps*.

LUCAS: You shouldn't let him get to you.

NEALE: Don't worry, I won't.

PARRY: Hey, you don't want to waste your time with him
– He's not interested in girls, if you know what I mean.

LUCAS: You're sick in the head. Do you know that, Parry?

PARRY: Give us a kiss.

(*SULLIVAN enters the rest room.*)

SULLIVAN: Steve…

(*SULLIVAN and LUCAS exit.*)

NEALE: What is it that makes you behave like such a cretin?

PARRY: Too much sex.

NEALE: Who with? Yourself?

(*NEALE leaves the rest room, she crosses through the office into the SEA.*)

K S: (*To LEONELLA.*) If it hadn't been for your damn photographs we'd've been out of here long ago. They're only keeping us here because of you…and that ignorant American. The jet lag, I can live with. The aggravation, I can live with. But I can't stand having my time wasted… And they confiscated my mobile phone.

NEALE: (*To MANGBETU.*) *Vous vous sentez vraiment bien? Puis-je vous aider?*

(*SULLIVAN and LUCAS bring DION into the SEA.*)

(*To SULLIVAN.*) I was just seing if she needed anything.

(*NEALE exits. SULLIVAN and LUCAS leave DION and exit.*)

DION: I'm mad.

K S: I already told you that.

DION: No, seriously. I just seen some doctor, airport doctor. I'm insane. And I got a certificate to prove it.

LEONELLA: What will happen to you?

DION: They're gonna contact my commanding officer in Germany. I'll get sent back there, I guess.

LEONELLA: It's my fault –

DION: No… No… Forget it…

K S: Do you realise that I've been here three hours now.

(*K S takes out a calculator.*)

DION: I guess you missed your competition.

(*LEONELLA looks at her watch, she shrugs resignedly.*)

LEONELLA: Unless there's a miracle.

K S: One thousand, one hundred and seventy pounds, thirty-six pence.

DION: Now what you goin' on about?

K S: By my calculation the Home Office now owe me one thousand, one hundred and seventy pounds, thirty-six pence.

DION: How d'you work that out?

K S: Three hundred and ninety pounds, twelve pence per hour.

DION: For what?

K S: My consultancy fee plus loss of potential revenue.

LEONELLA: (*To DION.*) Dion, what do you do there? In Germany?

DION: Ground crew – F-18s. McDonald Douglas Hornet, baddest bird in the sky. I'm a technician with an attitude problem.

LEONELLA: What do you mean?

DION: I'd rather be a football player.

K S: American football…

DION: Yeah, American football.

K S: Cricket is a far superior game.

DION: Cricket? What's cricket?

K S: Philistine.

DION: Cricket's for faggots.

K S: What! I'd like to see you deal with a cricket ball hurtling towards you at over a hundred miles per hour. That takes courage.

DION: Crap! They don't even notice when it hits 'em, they're so damn fat. You need muscle for football.

K S: Muscle and padding… You don't know what you're talking about. The United States of America – The country that made national institutions of rounders and netball.

DION: You're beginnin' to get on my nerves again, you know that.

K S: You have got us all into a great deal of trouble. It's your fault they're keeping us here. And her… (*Indicating LEONELLA.*) stupid photographs.

DION: You'd've preferred it if I'd showed 'em the photographs, is that it?… No, I didn't think so. What happened to those photographs anyhow?

LEONELLA: I don't know, I thought you had them…

DION: (*To K S.*) You took 'em, didn't you? (*To MANGBETU.*) He take them photographs from you?

MANGBETU: Yes.

DION: Give 'em back.

LEONELLA: I don't want them.

DION: You could still get through. You don't know for certain if they found out about the photographs...

LEONELLA: I don't want them.

DION: Well, he can't have 'em. (*Holding out a hand.*) Here.

K S: Not a chance.

DION: I ain't messin'... You heard... C'mon, hand 'em over, Or you want us to tell 'em you was behind the whole idea?

K S: You think they'll believe you...

DION: You think they'll believe you? Now, I suggest you give me them photographs, before I'm forced to take 'em.

K S: Alright... Here... Have your revolting photographs.

(*K S throws the photographs at DION.*)

DION: You know, you remind me of a guy I met once on his way to hospital.

LEONELLA: Stop it... Please.

(*LEONELLA picks up the pieces of the photographs. She sits back down.*)

LEONELLA: (*To K S.*) Will you tell them?

DION: He won't say shit, he didn't want no one to see the damn things in the first place. Besides, he ain't got the nerve. And he sure as hell won't say nothin' now.

K S: Oh, is that right.

DION: Yes. You're an accessory to the smuggling of obscene material.

K S: No I am not.

DION: Oh yes you are. You were the one destroyed the evidence.

K S: It was for the good of the country.

DION: Bullshit!

LEONELLA: The negatives are still in Spain anyway.

DION: Good old Hugo...

(*DION indicates that K S should kiss his arse.*)

K S: You have no respect, do you... Absolutely no respect.

(*LUCAS enters the SEA.*)

LUCAS: (*To DION.*) Mr Stanley...

DION: You got my bulbs?

LUCAS: Yes.

DION: And…

LUCAS: The bulbs we confiscated earlier today are tulip bulbs.

DION: Congratulations, man.

> (*DION holds his hand out for the bulbs.*)

LUCAS: Technically, Her Majesty's Customs are not allowed to return plant material brought into the country without a plant health certificate. But…

> (*LUCAS hands DION the bulbs.*)

DION: Tulip bulbs, tulip bulbs… So, what happens now?

LUCAS: We're going to pick up your bags, then you'll be escorted to your flight back to Germany.

DION: That it? I'm goin' right?

LUCAS: Yes. Sorry…

> (*PHURBU bows to DION, DION bows back.*)

DION: (*To MANGBETU.*) Nice meetin' you, madam. (*To K S.*) You, if you're ever in the States, don't look me up.

K S: I won't.

> (*DION hands his football to LEONELLA then exits with LUCAS. Lights down on airport. The tangka and three lords of the cemeteries appear on the top level. The tangka and lords of the cemeteries fade from view, it is two hours later. LEONELLA, MANGBETU and K S sit silently in the SEA, PHURBU stands downstage. SULLIVAN is in the office.*)

PHURBU: To continue with the parable of Sukyi Nyima…

> (*BARRATT enters the rest room, she is drinking a glass of gin. She is tipsy.*)

The Queen, Rigngen Bhumo, (*He indicates BARRATT.*) has grown jealous that she is no longer the 'fat of the heart' –

K S: The what?

PHURBU: The…apple of the eye, to the king.

> (*PARRY enters the office.*)

PARRY: That flight to Luanda.

SULLIVAN: What about it?

PARRY: It's well past their scheduled departure time.

SULLIVAN: They're not leaving here until we find out what the Home Office want us to do with that Chinese asylum application. They know that.

> (*PARRY notices BARRATT.*)

PARRY: Is she pissed?

SULLIVAN: I don't know.

(*SULLIVAN crosses into rest room. PARRY follows him.*)

SULLIVAN: (*To BARRATT.*) I told you to have a couple of drinks. Not get plastered.

PARRY: It's not every day you get bitten by an irate African-American. Tell you what, I'll shut her in the cleaners' cupboard if you want. If she's an embarrassment, I mean.

(*The telephone rings in the office, PARRY goes to answer it. SULLIVAN reaches for BARRATT's glass which she pulls away from him.*)

SULLIVAN: Give it to me.

(*SULLIVAN snatches the glass from BARRATT. PARRY crosses into rest room.*)

PARRY: (*To SULLIVAN.*) It's for you.

BARRATT: Dave…

(*SULLIVAN empties the glass into the sink and returns to the office. BARRATT follows him. PARRY remains in the rest room where he makes a phone call on the payphone.*)

Dave…

(*SULLIVAN answers the phone.*)

SULLIVAN: Dave Sullivan… Yes… Right. Will do. (*SULLIVAN hangs up.*) Your terrorist suspect has been in prison in Bilbao for the last three weeks. So you better get in there and apologize to Miss Corvera.

BARRATT: I wasn't to know.

SULLIVAN: Did I say you were?

BARRATT: (*Aggressively.*) You make it sound as if it's my fault. You were only too pleased when you thought you might get the praise for bringing in a terrorist.

SULLIVAN: What the bloody hell's got into you?

BARRATT: You. Touching her up. You're all over her.

SULLIVAN: All over who?

BARRATT: Our new, star attraction.

SULLIVAN: Susan?

BARRATT: Oh, it's 'Susan' now, is it?

SULLIVAN: Don't be so bloody pathetic.

BARRATT: I think this promotion has gone straight to your trousers.

SULLIVAN: You what?

BARRATT: It's put your libido into orbit. All I ever got from you was a quick grope and an invitation to watch Yorkshire county sodding cricket club in the Huntley and Palmers cup –

SULLIVAN: Benson and Hedges.

BARRATT: Benson and sodding Hedges, then…! Now… Now, all of a sudden, the woman of your wet dreams turns up and it's chocolates for her and extra strong mints for you to hide your bad breath.

SULLIVAN: I gave her a toffee. One pissing toffee!

BARRATT: I'm not good enough for you now, is that it? Well let me tell you, you won't get a better offer. You'll only make a fool of yourself with her. I know her sort.

SULLIVAN: Give it a rest woman. Honestly, you've got a mind like a bloody sewer.

BARRATT: Don't talk to me like that.

SULLIVAN: I'll talk to you how I bloody like. Now, pull yourself together or that's it.

BARRATT: (*Mockingly.*) Oh, someone help me before I desolve into tears.

SULLIVAN: Stop wasting my time and get on with your work – if you're capable.

BARRATT: I want her off the team.

SULLIVAN: Oh, you do, do you… Well, I got news for you – I make the decisions round here. When I want your advice I'll ask for it… I don't know why you didn't stay in the bloody police force.

BARRATT: I left the police force because I was sexually harrassed.

SULLIVAN: Well all I can say is they must've been bloody desperate. (*Pause – realizing he's gone too far.*) Listen, I'm sorry. Let's stop this. (*He puts his arms around her.*) I didn't mean nothing. You know what I'm like when I lose my rag. I'll make it up to you. (*He kisses her.*) Promise.
(*NEALE enters the office.*)

BARRATT: Get off! You're like a dirty old man sometimes. (*Notices NEALE.*) What are you staring at?
(*NEALE exits. LUCAS enters the office with a fax. He gives the fax to SULLIVAN.*)

SULLIVAN: (*As he reads.*) Campbell… (*To LUCAS.*) Tell Susan I want a word with her will you.

(*LUCAS crosses to the office door and opens it.*)

LUCAS: (*Calling out of the office.*) Susan… Sullivan wants you.

(*NEALE enters the office.*)

SULLIVAN: Sus… Someone's contacted a lawyer, name of Campbell, about the Zairean. He's claiming her detention's unlawful. Do you know anything about it?

NEALE: No.

SULLIVAN: I don't want to back down on this one. Find out what's going on. And watch yourself with Campbell, he's a devious bastard, he'll try and have you any way he can over this.

(*NEALE goes to leave.*)

Where you going?

NEALE: To see this solicitor.

SULLIVAN: You mean he's at the airport?

NEALE: I think so.

LUCAS: He's at the police station, been here all day.

SULLIVAN: Right… You'd better ring his office first, anyway. See what they've got to say. Number's on the fax.

NEALE: I'll just get my notes.

(*NEALE crosses to the rest room to collect her files.*)

BARRATT: (*To SULLIVAN.*) She must've told him… Who else could it be? Dave, we were the only ones who knew about her. I didn't notify him… Did you?

SULLIVAN: Give it a rest, woman, it's her husband, he must be here. It'll be him who got hold of Campbell.

(*NEALE re-enters the office.*)

(*To BARRATT.*) Are you going to leave that Spanish woman in there all night?

BARRATT: Yes.

SULLIVAN: (*To NEALE.*) You would say wouldn't you, if you knew anything about this lawyer…

NEALE: Of course.

(*SULLIVAN lays his hand affectionately on NEALE's back, then exits. NEALE makes a phone call. BARRATT goes into the rest room.*)

PARRY: Alright, Rowena?

BARRATT: He couldn't even be bothered to come for a
   drink – Had to stay up here and play Guru to his bloody
   precious Susan… She just sits there fluttering her eyelashes,
   yes David, no David, three sodding bags full David. She'll
   never last here, you know. You should have heard her
   this afternoon when that Zairean started playing up. (*In a
   pathetic tone.*) 'What am I meant to do?'
   (*BARRATT exits. SULLIVAN enters the SEA.*)

SULLIVAN: Senorita de Corvera. If you'd like to come with
   me. Everything's been sorted out. You can enter the
   country now.

LEONELLA: But I've missed my competition.

SULLIVAN: What competition?

LEONELLA: The dance competition I came here for.

SULLIVAN: Yes… Well, anyway… Enjoy the sights
   – Buckingham Palace, Tower of London, Kew Gardens…
   Lords, the Oval…

LEONELLA: Why did you keep me here?

SULLIVAN: I can't discuss that, I'm afraid… Well, do you want
   to go through or not?

LEONELLA: No. I'm taking the first flight back to Spain –
   Anywhere in Spain. Can you arrange a flight for me?

SULLIVAN: I wish you people'd make your minds up…
   Alright, come with me.
   (*SULLIVAN and LEONELLA exit.*)

PHURBU: Since Sukyi Nyima has come the King no longer
   chooses to spend time with his Queen. In her jealous anger
   Rigngen Bhumo throws poison on Sukyi Nyima. But she
   soon notices that the poison has had no ill effect. Rigngen
   Bhumo learns of the rosary beads that protect Sukyi Nyima
   and lures them away from her. She again tries her poison.
   And this time Sukyi Nyima falls ill and the King turns
   against her.
   (*BARRATT enters the office. NEALE gets up from her desk and
   crosses to a filing cabinet.*)

BARRATT: You told Campbell about the Zairean, didn't you?

NEALE: No… Anyway, what does it matter who contacted
   him? It's done now.

(*BARRATT picks up NEALE's bag and looks inside. BARRATT pulls out the pearl necklace from the bag and puts it in a drawer of the desk – NEALE does not see her do this.*)

BARRATT: Some people just can't take the pressure. All they can do is mess up other peoples hard work and follow senior officers around like little lost sheep.

NEALE: (*Dejectedly.*) Why are you doing this?

BARRATT: Doing what? I was just talking about declining standards in the immigration service. Especially the women they send us.

NEALE: I've got work to do.

(*NEALE turns to go. SULLIVAN enters the office.*)

SULLIVAN: Susan –

(*NEALE ignores him. She exits.*)

What's wrong with Susan?… Have you been having a go at her? You bloody have…

(*SULLIVAN exits. BARRATT picks up a framed photograph from SULLIVAN's desk and smashes it on the desk. PARRY crosses to the office from the rest room.*)

PARRY: I hope for your sake that's not his signed photograph of Freddy Truman.

(*BARRATT looks at the photograph.*)

BARRATT: It's Illingworth, his dog.

(*BARRATT hides the photo frame under some papers on the desk. As she does so she cuts herself on the glass from the frame. SULLIVAN re-enters the office.*)

SULLIVAN: I want you to apologize to Susan when she comes back.

BARRATT: Susan Neale is the only one who could've told Campbell about the Zairean. Her husband isn't here, no one's asked for a passenger list, I went down to the desk. Dave, she as good as admitted it to me…You're going to end up looking pretty stupid when the Assistant Director finds out you've got a mole.

(*LUCAS enters the office.*)

LUCAS: Dave.

SULLIVAN: Yes…

LUCAS: We're going to have to back down on the removal of the Zairean. The Assistant Director's office don't want it to go before a judge. We're to grant her temporary admission.

SULLIVAN: What?

LUCAS: I've just spoken with them.

SULLIVAN: You're not dealing with the Zairean.

LUCAS: You asked me to keep an eye on things – And I didn't have anything else to do.

SULLIVAN: So you just decided you'd speak to the Assistant Director about it. Thanks, Steve. I was trying to keep it quiet.

LUCAS: You got your promotion, didn't you? What do you care…

SULLIVAN: I care about being made to look like a prat. What's wrong with you?

LUCAS: Nothing's wrong with me.

SULLIVAN: Where's the directive?

LUCAS: What?

SULLIVAN: Where's the directive saying we're to grant her temporary admission?

(*NEALE enters.*)

LUCAS: In the office.

SULLIVAN: Get it, then.

(*LUCAS exits.*)

Susan, have you got any idea how Campbell found out about the Zairean yet?

NEALE: Afraid not.

SULLIVAN: Well, what have you found out?

NEALE: I'm waiting for his office to call back.

(*SULLIVAN crosses to his desk. He picks up part of the broken frame.*)

SULLIVAN: How did this happen?

BARRATT: It fell off.

SULLIVAN: Fell off! Don't take the piss…

(*LUCAS re-enters the office.*)

LUCAS: Here's your directive.

BARRATT: (*To SULLIVAN.*) How many times do I have to tell you – She contacted Campbell.

SULLIVAN: Susan…

LUCAS: It wasn't her.

SULLIVAN: (*To NEALE.*) I trusted you.

NEALE: I didn't contact any lawyer.

SULLIVAN: Just get out of my sight.

LUCAS: She's telling the truth… It was me. I spoke to him.

SULLIVAN: Don't be such a bloody martyr.

LUCAS: I'm not being a martyr.

SULLIVAN: You're just trying to protect her.

LUCAS: I'm not. I've had enough. I'm not prepared to stand by and listen to you dictate immigration policy any more.

SULLIVAN: What the hell are you talking about?

LUCAS: The Zairean… All of them.

SULLIVAN: If, and I mean 'if', she is finally to be removed, it will only be after her case has been dealt with cooly and calmly at port level, and after the Home Office have given her request mature consideration –

LUCAS: Don't spout at me. You weren't even going to let her claim asylum. You're so full of your own importance, posturing, acting like you're some kind of almighty tin god –

SULLIVAN: That's it. You've gone too far.

LUCAS: Me!

(*LUCAS turns his back and exits.*)

SULLIVAN: (*Calling after LUCAS.*) You are in big trouble! You hear me? Big trouble!

(*PARRY goes to speak.*)

Shut up… I'll have that queer bastard for this.

(*SULLIVAN notices BARRATT is holding her finger.*)

What's wrong with you?

BARRATT: Nothing. I've cut my finger, that's all.

SULLIVAN: (*To PARRY.*) Rob, Take her (*Indicating NEALE.*) into the rest room. And don't let her out of your sight.

NEALE: I haven't done anything. Do you think I'm going to run away?

SULLIVAN: Just get in there.

(*PARRY and NEALE go to the rest room. PARRY picks up the payphone and makes a call.*)

PHURBU: So the wise minister attempted to save Sukyi Nyima's life by offering the blood from his own neck. But the King was now convinced of Sukyi Nyima's guilt and ordered an executioner to take her to the cremation ground where he is to leave her for the wild animals to eat. However, when the wild animals arrive they eat the executioner and leave Sukyi Nyima to meditate on the teachings of the hermit saint Dhangsong. Sukyi Nyima now realises she must go amongst the people preaching her religion.

SULLIVAN: I'll be bloody glad when they get the quickie system up and running. Quick yes or no from the adjudicator and that'd be it. Wouldn't've had all this bloody messing about today. Their feet wouldn't've touched the bloody ground. Straight back out again, no pissing about... (*Turning towards the rest room.*) Parry... (*SULLIVAN goes to the rest room.*)

Parry...

(*SULLIVAN sees that PARRY is on the phone.*)

PARRY: (*Hesitant.*) It's the Home Office.

SULLIVAN: Why are you using the payphone? Give it here. (*SULLIVAN takes the phone.*)

(*Slowing as he speaks.*) Chief Immigration Officer Sulli– (*SULLIVAN listens for a moment, then moves the phone away from his ear and stares at the receiver in disbelief. He trepidatiously returns the phone to his ear and listens again for a short time with a pained, incredulous expression. He then hands the phone back to PARRY. PARRY hangs up.*)

SULLIVAN: Why, Parry?

PARRY: I write them.

SULLIVAN: You write filthy, degenerate, pornographic phone messages?

PARRY: I try to, yes.

SULLIVAN: I don't believe I'm hearing this.

PARRY: There was an advert.

SULLIVAN: I know. I've bloody seen them.

PARRY: No. For writers. It was in the paper.

SULLIVAN: So now you spend all day listening to these...these things.

PARRY: Just checking out the competition.

SULLIVAN: You idiot.

PARRY: My messages are very popular.

SULLIVAN: I'm surrounded by drunks, informers, vandals, and sex maniacs. God help the civil service.

PARRY: Everyone does a bit of moonlighting –

SULLIVAN: Shut up, Parry. I'm not interested. Listen, I'm going into the SEA, if the Home Office do get in touch

– No, we can't wait any longer. Leave her for a minute,
get back in there (*Indicating the office.*) and ring them. Say
we urgently need a yes or no on the Chinese asylum case
or we're going to have to put him in detention and wait
till Christ knows when for the next flight out. I'll get that
Zairean out of the way.

(*SULLIVAN returns to the office, PARRY follows him. PARRY picks
up a phone and punches in a number. SULLIVAN exits, BARRATT
exits after him. SULLIVAN and BARRATT enter the SEA.*)

(*To MANGBETU.*) Come on, you're coming with me. (*Notices
K S.*) What are you still doing here?

K S: Can I go?

SULLIVAN: I'll sort you out when I've seen to this lady.

MANGBETU: Where are you taking me?

SULLIVAN: I'm going to hand you over to some people who'll
find you accommodation.

MANGBETU: I want to see my husband.

SULLIVAN: The refugee arrivals group have got all your
details, they'll help you find him.

MANGBETU: No, I don't believe you. You're going to send me
back –

SULLIVAN: Your request for asylum has been provisionally
granted. All we need to do is make an appointment to see
you in a couple of weeks' time.

MANGBETU: No.

(*PARRY concludes his phone call. He exits from the office and
enters the SEA.*)

SULLIVAN: You're doing yourself no favours.

MANGBETU: I want my husband. I won't go until I have seen
my husband.

SULLIVAN: There's already a lawyer here at the airport. He'll
help with any problems you might have. You'll see your
husband... Come on... Come with me.

MANGBETU: No.

SULLIVAN: Do you want me to drag you out, because I will if
I have to.

(*SULLIVAN waits for a moment, then goes to grab
MANGBETU.*)

MANGBETU: No. No!

PARRY: Careful, Dave. Campbell's out there remember.
Perhaps Rowena… I mean, it might be better if a female
officer did it.

SULLIVAN: You're right. Rowena – Get her up will you.

(*BARRATT crosses to MANGBETU and grabs her under the
arms.*)

MANGBETU: Leave me… Leave me!

(*BARRATT attempts to pull MANGBETU up but does it with
such drunken enthusiasm that as she lifts her she stumbles and
slams MANGBETU down on the floor, falling on top of her.
MANGBETU cries out in pain. SULLIVAN pulls BARRATT off
and throws her to the floor.*)

SULLIVAN: Are you bloody mad!

(*SULLIVAN and PARRY tend to MANGBETU.*)

MANGBETU: *Ne m'y renvoyez pas. Ne m'y renvoyez pas.*

PARRY: Is she alright?

SULLIVAN: How do I know.

BARRATT: Dave…

(*SULLIVAN turns to look at BARRATT.*)

SULLIVAN: (*To PARRY.*) Get her out of here. And get Neale. (*He
helps MANGBETU to sit up.*) Come on…

(*SULLIVAN pulls BARRATT to her feet. PHURBU goes to help
MANGBETU.*)

Leave her alone. (*To MANGBETU.*) *C'est bien. Tout ira bien.*

(*PARRY leads BARRATT into the office, then goes to the rest
room.*)

PARRY: He wants you. SEA – Trouble with the Zairean
woman.

(*NEALE and PARRY cross through the office into the SEA.*)

SULLIVAN: *Pouvez-vous vous lever?*

NEALE: What happened?

(*SULLIVAN and NEALE help MANGBETU to stand.*)

SULLIVAN: There's been an accident. Take her to the PMI…
Talk to her. Persuade her everything's alright, she'll listen
to you…

NEALE: *Nous irons voir le docteur. Tout sera bien vous voyerez votre
mari. Personne ne vous y renvoyera.*

(*NEALE exits with MANGBETU. SULLIVAN and PARRY follow
them out.*)

PHURBU: In time Rigngen Bhumo begins to feel remorse for her actions, she confesses her sins and offers the pearl rosary beads as a repentance.

(*SULLIVAN and PARRY enter the rest room and cross through it into the office.*)

PARRY: What if she loses the baby?

SULLIVAN: Don't ask stupid questions.

PARRY: But if she loses it –

SULLIVAN: What do you expect me to do? It wasn't me who bloody jumped on her.

PARRY: You could've stopped her.

SULLIVAN: It was your bloody idea.

(*SULLIVAN notices BARRATT.*)

BARRATT: Dave…

SULLIVAN: Get out of my sight.

(*NEALE enters the office.*)

NEALE: None of this need have happened if we'd just been straight with her… She's going to have to stay with the doctor for a while, in case there's a miscarriage. Is it alright if I try to find a contact number or address for her husband?

SULLIVAN: Whatever.

(*NEALE sits at a desk and begins to use the computer.*)

(*To BARRATT.*) I thought I told you to get out.

(*BARRATT opens a drawer to take some things out, NEALE sees her necklace in the drawer. BARRATT takes the necklace out and hands it to NEALE.*)

BARRATT: That's yours. I was only messing about. Sorry.

NEALE: Why?

BARRATT: You… And Dave.

NEALE: What are you talking about?

BARRATT: You were flirting with him.

NEALE: With him! You must be joking.

BARRATT: It was Steve, wasn't it, who rang the lawyer…

NEALE: I don't know. I talked to him about Mangbetu, I even asked him if there was something I could do to prevent her removal. But I didn't dare do anything.

SULLIVAN: This place has been like a bloody madhouse today. It's not always like this, you know.

(*BARRATT exits.*)

PARRY: Er… That Chinese asylum case… We're to get him out. They don't want no trouble with the Chinese, not with all the shit flying about Hong Kong. Gave me a right earful about getting on with it, then told me I wasn't to do anything until they'd spoken to you. There's civil service logic for you.

SULLIVAN: When did you find this out?

PARRY: Five minutes ago.

SULLIVAN: Why the bloody hell didn't you say? God help me. Go and inform the crew they can get ready for departure. I'll see what the Home Office want then I'll get him to the plane.

(*PARRY exits. SULLIVAN punches a number into the telephone.*)

You might as well sign out when you've done that, the new shift'll be here in a minute.

NEALE: I've got to get Mangbetu's things and take them to the PMI. (*NEALE copies down some information from the computer.*) I'll ring her husband from there.

SULLIVAN: Fine. (*On the phone.*) Extension 2041, please…

(*NEALE exits. SULLIVAN turns his back and holds a discreet telephone conversation. NEALE enters the SEA on her way to the PMI.*)

K S: At last.

(*K S stands, he straightens his suit and tie.*)

NEALE: Pardon?

K S: I can go? Him…. (*He indicates the office.*) He said he would deal with me next.

NEALE: It's nothing to do with me I'm afraid.

K S: This… This is some kind of game to you. Do you enjoy aggravating people?

NEALE. (*Turning to go.*) Excuse me.

K S: No. I will not excuse you. I would like to know why it is that you are prepared to obstruct and delay honest, decent people when you, personally, have nothing to gain, either financially or otherwise.

NEALE: I don't know what you're getting at.

K S: I am 'getting at' the question of why you should choose to make things so difficult for me when it is of absolutely no consequence to you. What have I done?

NEALE: Nothing.

K S: So what is it about me?

NEALE: We have to be careful who we let into the UK.

K S: I agree, but I repeat, what is it about me?

    (*SULLIVAN enters the SEA.*)

SULLIVAN: Will you come with me please, Mr Tsering.

    (*NEALE exits.*)

K S: (*To SULLIVAN.*) You –

    (*SULLIVAN goes into the interview area, PHURBU follows him in. K S crosses and stands listening impatiently at the door.*)

SULLIVAN: Sit down, please. I'm afraid your request for political asylum has been turned down by the Home Office, Mr Tsering. We're going to have to return you to Angola.

PHURBU: But they will send me back to China… Why?

SULLIVAN: You are what we refer to as a third country removal. Meaning that you've claimed asylum in one country, decided you didn't like it and then come here.

PHURBU: But I haven't claimed asylum in Angola. It would be pointless… How can you know?

SULLIVAN: You've entered Britain from another country, that's all the information we need. Your plane will be leaving in about half an hour.

PHURBU: You must not send me back.

SULLIVAN: Would it be possible for you to move to another part of China?

PHURBU: I'm not Chinese. Can't you understand?

SULLIVAN: I understand, alright. But I'm afraid there's nothing I can do. You want us to let you enter this country because you don't like what happened to your brother and because you said something you shouldn't have – What do we get in return? A lot of people who come here don't give a damn about Britain. Some of them are downright, bloody rude. Do you think that's right? Do you?

    (*PHURBU shrugs.*)

SULLIVAN: Britain's a small country, it's overcrowded as it is –

PHURBU: Why are you telling me this?

SULLIVAN: I'm simply explaining our position… We take our share of refugees, but we can't take everyone. Where would we put them? We've probably taken too many as it is – From Ugandan Asians to Bosnian Muslims… But it doesn't stop there. I mean, over the next few years, for example, we expect a lot of economic migrants from Hong Kong to try to enter the country illegally. It's going to be very difficult for us to stop them, but we have to do it. Otherwise… Who knows what might happen with the triads and all the undesirable elements that might get in.

PHURBU: What has this got to do with me?

SULLIVAN: Sometimes decent people get snared. We can't help that. People like you. You're different, you're an educated man. How many languages do you speak? Tibetan, English, Chinese – Mandarin, Guoyu…

(*PHURBU does not answer.*)

Someone like you might fit in.

PHURBU: What do you mean?

SULLIVAN: It'd probably be easy for you to get a job in London, in a restaurant, or any number of Chinese businesses.

PHURBU: You want me to spy for you?

SULLIVAN: That's not what I said.

PHURBU: This is exactly what I was trying to escape from.

SULLIVAN: You've completely misunderstood me.

PHURBU: Have I?

SULLIVAN: Britain is a democracy.

PHURBU: But this is the same as the Work Units and Neighbourhood Committees in Lhasa, everyone spying on each other, afraid to say or do anything.

SULLIVAN: I'm not here to argue with you. It's a waste of my time, and yours. (*Pause.*) You have to put yourself first. Isn't that what you did when you made the decision to come here?

PHURBU: I don't know.

(*SULLIVAN stands. K S returns to his seat.*)

SULLIVAN: Think about it… You've got about five minutes before I take you to the plane.

(*SULLIVAN ushers PHURBU back into the SEA.*)

I'll get someone to take you through, Mr Ramalingham.

(*SULLIVAN goes into the office. JANET MILLER enters the office – she is working on the following shift.*)

MILLER: You still here?

SULLIVAN: Janet, hello. Has the shift changed? I'm a bit behind. Would you do something for me? (*SULLIVAN hands MILLER a form.*) Show Mr Ramalingham through customs, will you. He might give you a bit of earache, but he's no trouble really. He's in the SEA.

MILLER: Passport?

SULLIVAN: Hasn't got it – That's what the problem was. He's been here quite a time. Apologize to him... Hold on, better take these.

(*SULLIVAN hands MILLER K S's phone, Psion organiser and driving license. MILLER enters the SEA.*)

MILLER: Mr... (*She looks at the driving license.*) K S Ramalingham.

(*Neither K S nor PHURBU move.*)

Which one of you is Mr Ramalingham?

K S: (*To PHURBU.*) Goodbye.

(*They shake hands.*)

Don't wait for me. I may be some time.

(*PHURBU stares at him.*)

I would be grateful (*K S writes a number on a piece of notepaper.*) if you could ring this number when you are through. Just to let my friends know that you've seen me here.

MILLER: I don't think so. (*MILLER: takes the note.*) Come along, Mr Ramaligham.

(*PHURBU looks at K S, K S gesticulates that PHURBU should go. MILLER gives PHURBU K S's confiscated phone, organiser and driving license. PHURBU turns to K S once again.*)

K S: Goodbye.

(*MILLER leads PHURBU out.*)

MILLER: We're very sorry for detaining you. I hope you understand that he have to be very careful...

(*MILLER and PHURBU exit. K S knocks an imaginary cricket ball for six. SULLIVAN enters the SEA, he looks at K S, then looks inside the interview area. He returns to the SEA and stares at K S again, a look of sudden realization spreading over his face. The door to the SEA from the arrivals floor bursts opens, PARRY enters with PHURBU and MILLER. SULLIVAN sighs a huge sigh of relief. K S adds up some figures on his pocket calculator.*)

K S: Two thousand, three hundred and forty-eight pounds, seventeen pence, down the drain.

(*Lights down on stage. Spot on PHURBU.*)

PHURBU: (*To audience.*) What happened to us all?…
Mr Ramalingham soon convinced the immigration authorities that what happened at the airport was just a momentary aberration. He was recently elected as a Conservative councillor in Birmingham. Dion is now the manager of his brother's Garden Centre. Leonella is still dancing – The MP in the photographs recently resigned. And Mangbetu… She lives with her husband in Dalston. They have found it very hard to adjust to life in Britain, especially since their daughter was born… What about the story of Sukyi Nyima? Well, after parting from Rigugen Bhumo, Dawe Senge made Sukyi Nyima his Queen. Together they had a son, Nyime Senge – Sun's Lion – who became King in his turn and continued to spread Buddhism throughout the land.

DION: (*Voice off.*) And that's it?

PHURBU: Yes.

K S: (*Voice off.*) What did you expect, the Lone Ranger?

PHURBU: Oh – And where am I now? – Who knows…

(*Lights down on PHURBU. The tangka once again appears and four lords of the cemeteries, perform a dance called 'Dhurdak Cham'. Towards the end of the dance there is the sound of an over-flying aircraft and a slow fade back into the airport reality, the immigration officers enter as if at the start of a new shift – but instead they are joined by the detainees and together they throw a handful of tsampa into the air to propitiate the gods.*)

(*The End.*)

CRUSADE

Characters

MAHMOUD SAID
works for a vehicle hire company in Akko (Acre), Israel, in his twenties

MICHAEL LEACH
President of the First National Melbourne Bank. Deirdre's husband. English, fifty

DEIRDRE LEACH
a financial adviser. Michael's wife. Australian, mid-forties

CLIVE GREEN
an actor. English, thirty

AYESHA MIRZA
an expert in oriental antiquities, specialising in Islamic Art, Indian family, born and educated in Britain, late twenties

FRAN STOTT
a new age traveller. British, thirties

BARRY HARRINGTON
a Rastafarian. Born and brought up in London, in his thirties

A PALESTINIAN
on a bicycle

Crusade was first performed at the Theatre Royal Stratford East on 11th April 1994 with the following cast:

BARRY,   Burt Caesar
MICHAEL,   Peter Ellis
DEIRDRE,   Trudie Goodwin
CLIVE,   Marcus Hutton
MAHMOOD,   Ben Joseph
FRAN,   Kate Lonergan
AYESHA,   Tara Shaw
PALESTINIAN - David Cauchi

Director,   Jeff Teare
Designer,   Jenny Tiramani
Lighting Consultant,   Richard Moffatt
Assistant Director,   Indhu Rubasingham

One

Early 1994.

A semi-desert, mountain track in the Israeli-occupied West Bank somewhere between Nablus and Jerusalem. An arid landscape: jagged rock, sand, scarce vegetation. In the rock at the rear of the stage is the concealed entrance to a cave. The sun is beating down, it is very hot – about midday. A PALESTINIAN on a bicycle passes along the track and exits. The sound of a labouring engine. A mini-bus with Israeli number plates drives into view and judders to a halt. The mini-bus is a wreck – covered in dents and scratches, the bodywork and windows filthy with dust. Inside the bus are a driver, MAHMOUD, and his six passengers: MICHAEL, DEIRDRE, FRAN, BARRY, CLIVE, and AYESHA. The PALESTINIAN cycles back on stage, he stops and stares at the bus. MAHMOUD winds his window down, the PALESTINIAN gestures to MAHMOUD to see if he needs any help – MAHMOUD succeeds in restarting the engine and waves the PALESTINIAN away. The PALESTINIAN exits. The engine cuts. After several attempts to re-start the mini-bus MAHMOUD throws open the driver's door and gets out. He opens the bonnet of the mini-bus and peers inside. The passenger door opens and DEIRDRE steps out – she is wearing a sun hat.

DEIRDRE: I knew it!
> (*MICHAEL and BARRY climb out of the bus.*)
MICHAEL: (*Pointing after the PALESTINIAN.*) Who was that?
MAHMOUD: I don't know.
> (*MICHAEL surveys the area through his binoculars.*)
DEIRDRE: I knew this would happen. (*To MAHMOUD.*) Where are we?
MAHMOUD: I'm not sure.
DEIRDRE: What do you mean, you're not sure?
MAHMOUD: I've never been this way before.
DEIRDRE: You're a driver, aren't you? You must have some idea.
MAHMOUD: I usually work in the office.
DEIRDRE: Are you telling me this is the first time you've done this journey?
MAHMOUD: This journey… I've done five, maybe six times.
DEIRDRE: That's something, at least.

MAHMOUD: But I never drove before.

DEIRDRE: Oh, terrific. You hear that, Michael?

MICHAEL: (*Still looking through his binoculars.*) I heard.

DEIRDRE: This whole thing's a bloody farce.

MICHAEL: (*Puts his binoculars down – to MAHMOUD.*) Mr Said, I suggest you get this heap of scrap metal going. I have already had enough of my time wasted today.

(*MAHMOUD pulls out a tool box from under the driver's seat. MICHAEL looks out through his binoculars again. BARRY crosses to MAHMOUD.*)

BARRY: (*To MAHMOUD.*) Can I help?

MAHMOUD: Do you know anything about diesel engines?

BARRY: No.

MAHMOUD: Then you can't help, can you.

(*MAHMOUD returns to the engine. BARRY sits on a rock, he opens his shoulder bag and takes out a book of contemporary poetry – Derek Walcott – and starts reading. CLIVE and AYESHA get out of the bus. DEIRDRE stands watching them.*)

CLIVE: I don't like it here. It's too hot. What if there are snakes?… I bet we end up having to push it.

AYESHA: Don't say things like that. Anyway, I thought you liked the sun.

CLIVE: I do, but not this kind of heat, it's oppressive. Reminds me of that film. What was it? Brilliant film… John Mills and Sylvia Syms – they had to push that ambulance across the desert. What's-his-name was a German spy… What was it called? They used it for that lager advert.

AYESHA: I can't remember – *Ice-Cold in Alex.*

CLIVE: That's it. Brilliant film. What was that actor's name? The spy… What I'd give to get a part in a film like that.

AYESHA: I thought you hated film.

CLIVE: The aesthetic is in the performance not the medium, Ayesha.

AYESHA: That's not what you said when that student turned you down for that Channel Four thing last year.

CLIVE: Thank you, I really needed to be reminded about that.

(*DEIRDRE crosses to CLIVE and AYESHA.*)

DEIRDRE: Shit to this, eh?

CLIVE: Life is as tedious as a twice told tale.

DEIRDRE: Come again?

CLIVE: Lewis. *King John...* Shakespeare.

DEIRDRE: Right.

CLIVE: (*Indicating MAHMOUD.*) I'll see if I can...do anything. (*CLIVE crosses to MAHMOUD and stands watching him work on the engine.*)

DEIRDRE: You on holiday?

AYESHA: No.

CLIVE: (*Calling across from where he is standing with MAHMOUD.*) Yes.

AYESHA: Sort of.

DEIRDRE: (*Indicating CLIVE.*) He your boyfriend?

CLIVE: (*Answering before AYESHA can deny it.*) Yes.

DEIRDRE: Where you from?

AYESHA: London. Where –

DEIRDRE: Melbourne. Deirdre Leach. Pleased to meet you. My husband's the cretin with the binoculars. Been in Haifa a couple of weeks. Thought we better do the Holy Land bit. You been out here before?

AYESHA: Yes. Clive hasn't.

DEIRDRE: I wanted to fly to Jerusalem, but he hates flying. Luxury air-conditioned coach... (*Turning to the mini-bus.*) Look at it. (*Indicating MAHMOUD.*) And as for him.

AYESHA: It's not his fault the coach went without us.

DEIRDRE: He works for them doesn't he?

AYESHA: Yes, but it wasn't him who gave us the wrong times.

DEIRDRE: It's him who got us lost.

AYESHA: I suppose so. Things have always been very well organized when I've been out here before, but it's all been a bit of a disaster this time. A car was meant to come for us yesterday, but no one showed up. Then we missed the coach. Now this.

DEIRDRE: What's this 'sort of' holiday you're on then?

AYESHA: I'm here to help a colleague of mine organize an exhibition in East Jerusalem.

DEIRDRE: We collect art, you know.

AYESHA: Really... What sort of thing?

DEIRDRE: Sculpture, fine art. We got heaps of stuff at home.

AYESHA: Such as?

DEIRDRE: Got a Modigliani.

AYESHA: Modigliani. That's wonderful.

(*FRAN gets out of the bus and stretches. She sits and plays a plainsong melody on her recorder.*)

DEIRDRE: Bloody hippy... So what's in this exhibition of yours?

AYESHA: Mostly ceramics, textiles, that kind of thing.

DEIRDRE: You never know, we might buy some off you.

AYESHA: I don't think so. They're antiquities. Some of the pieces date back to the twelfth century. They're not for sale, I'm afraid.

DEIRDRE: You some kind of expert?

AYESHA: You could say that.

DEIRDRE: Why didn't you fly straight to Jeruslaem?

AYESHA: Clive insisted on a couple of days by the Med. He doesn't feel he's had a holiday unless he's got sand in his underpants. I hate lying around doing nothing.

DEIRDRE: You don't like the beach?

AYESHA: No.

DEIRDRE: Me neither. Covered in bloody moles. Doctor says there's nothing to worry about. But you can't be too careful. Specially in heat like this. I never go out in the sun at home, just sit in my office and bask in the air conditioning.

AYESHA: What do you do?

DEIRDRE: I'm a financial adviser.

AYESHA: Sounds high powered.

DEIRDRE: Not really. Michael, my husband, he's the one with the power. He's President of the First National Melbourne Bank. Been there six years now.

AYESHA: Is that where you met him?

DEIRDRE: Christ, no. We've been married seventeen years. We were both working for the same bank in Adelaide.

AYESHA: He's not Australian –

DEIRDRE: No, English. Got a bit of French in him too somewhere, so he says.

(*CLIVE re-joins AYESHA and DEIRDRE.*)

CLIVE: I think this could take some time.

AYESHA: What's wrong with it?

CLIVE: No idea.

DEIRDRE: (*Deliberately – so that MAHMOUD overhears.*) He doesn't get it going in ten minutes, he'll have me to reckon with.
(*FRAN stops playing the recorder. MICHAEL crosses to DEIRDRE, AYESHA and CLIVE.*)

MICHAEL: (*To CLIVE – pointing something out.*) Over there.
(*CLIVE follows the line of MICHAEL's outstretched arm.*)

CLIVE: What?
(*MICHAEL hands his binoculars to CLIVE.*)

MICHAEL: In the fork of that tree.

CLIVE: (*Looking through binoculars.*) What tree?

MICHAEL: That bloody tree. Christ man, it's the only one up here.

AYESHA: What is it?

MICHAEL: A chaffinch.

AYESHA: A what?

DEIRDRE: (*To AYESHA.*) He was abused as a child – His Father used to take him bird watching.

MICHAEL: (*To CLIVE.*) *Fringilla coelebs.* Sexually dimorphic. You know, a lot of people make the mistake of thinking the chaffinch is a specifically European bird.

CLIVE: I can't see anything.

MICHAEL: Here.
(*MICHAEL snatches the binoculars back and peers through them.*)
He's gone.

DEIRDRE: Michael, go and get this death trap started.

MICHAEL: (*Ignoring DEIRDRE – to CLIVE.*) Listen… (*Imitating a chaffinch call.*) 'chwink-chwink, chwink-chwink'. Can you hear him?

CLIVE: I think so.

DEIRDRE: Michael –

MICHAEL: I don't know anything about engines, darling… Listen, I'm going to investigate that nest.

DEIRDRE: You shouldn't go wandering off.

MICHAEL: I'll be back before you can say *Corvus corone cornix.* And don't look at me like that.

DEIRDRE: Michael…
(*MICHAEL exits.*)
(*Calling after MICHAEL.*) What about my melanomas…

MICHAEL: (*Voice off.*) Put some sunblock on.

CLIVE: Back before you can say what?

DEIRDRE: I don't bloody know.

AYESHA: You don't share your husband's interest in ornithology –

DEIRDRE: Not exactly.

(*FRAN crosses to MAHMOUD. She watches MAHMOUD working on the engine for a moment.*)

FRAN: You don't know what you're doing, do you?… Get out the way. I spent the last six years in a bus up and down the A34. Go on – shift. Let me have a look… See, compression has to be high enough so that the temperature of the gas in the cylinders at the high compression point is sufficient to cause ignition… You do speak English, don't you?

MAHMOUD: Yes. I studied English. Not technical language though.

(*FRAN starts working on the engine.*)

FRAN: Are we lost?

MAHMOUD: Temporarily misplaced.

FRAN: Lost, then.

MAHMOUD: See that mountain…Ba'al Hazor. We're a few miles north of Ramallah. Exactly where north of Ramallah, I don't know, but…about an hour from Jerusalem… Will you stay in Jerusalem long?

FRAN: Don't know. Depends on money. Probably make my way to a kibbutz sooner or later.

(*DEIRDRE crosses to the bus. She leans inside, takes some sun cream from her bag and begins to apply it.*)

DEIRDRE: (*To MAHMOUD.*) You got five minutes left to get it started.

FRAN: It'll take as long as it takes.

DEIRDRE: I wasn't talking to you.

MAHMOUD: I'll radio for assistance.

DEIRDRE: You do that.

(*MAHMOUD goes to the driver's door and takes a mobile radio handset from its mounting.*)

You fancy him?

FRAN: No.

DEIRDRE: I've taken acid, you know.

FRAN: What?

DEIRDRE: Drugs.

FRAN: I'm not into drugs.

DEIRDRE: Is that right?

FRAN: I believe in exploring experiences that surpass normal understanding in a state of awareness. Not induced through drugs. I base my life on a unified cosmology of being – an interconnectedness between seen and unseen, outer and inner, reason beyond reason.

DEIRDRE: Drugs. You can't shut out the real world all your life.

FRAN: I don't take drugs. Didn't you hear a word I said.

DEIRDRE: You're a hippy, aren't you?

FRAN: No.

DEIRDRE: Why do you go round dressed like a cross between a peasant and a mirror ball, then?

FRAN: I'd take that as an insult if it came from an intelligent human being. Now, why don't you take that fried egg off your head and let me get on.

DEIRDRE: This hat was crafted by a top Sydney milliner to my own design.

FRAN: And you admit it!

DEIRDRE: Your parents must be heartbroken.

(*DEIRDRE gets into the mini-bus. CLIVE crosses to BARRY. MAHMOUD replaces the radio handset and takes out a map.*)

CLIVE: Good book?

BARRY: Derek Walcott.

CLIVE: (*Introducing himself.*) Clive Green.

(*CLIVE shakes BARRY's hand.*)

This is Ayesha.

(*BARRY acknowledges AYESHA. AYESHA joins them.*)

CLIVE: Ayesha – Derek. Derek – Ayesha.

BARRY: No, man. The book is by Derek Walcott. My name is Barry.

CLIVE: Oh, I see. Sorry.

BARRY: 'Broadening my horizons
Following the ghost
Travelling is my master
Giving me the most
I see all kinds of human life
Men who cheat and boast

But Travelling is my mistress
The one I love the most.'
Just passing through – How about you?

CLIVE: Holiday.

AYESHA: Work.

BARRY: I got sick and tired of London, grey London…

CLIVE: Do you do a lot of travelling?

BARRY: My life is a journey. The road is my book, and the book is my road.

AYESHA: You've been away from London a long time, then.

BARRY: About three days. I try not to measure time. I had enough of the Babylon shitstem. So I pack my bag, let the four winds carry I to Ethiopia. This is my beginning. I observe, I travel, and I read.

CLIVE: I could do with a good read myself.

(BARRY offers his book to CLIVE.)

No. No, it's alright.

(BARRY opens his bag and one by one produces a selection of books for CLIVE to choose from.)

BARRY: *The Fire Next Time* – James Baldwin. *The Autobiography of Malcolm X. London A to Z* – great illustrations, crap plot. *The History of Ethiopia. Bible.* Maya Angelou – *And Still I Rise.* Biography – John Barnes. You like football?

CLIVE: Er… I've seen *An Evening With Gary Lineker.*

(MAHMOUD crosses to within hearing distance of CLIVE, BARRY and AYESHA – he is checking out a map reference.)

BARRY: So who you support?

CLIVE: Er… Arsenal.

BARRY: I hate Arsenal.

CLIVE: Well I don't really support them. I don't support anyone. My uncle took me to see Leyton Orient once. Christ, I'll go mad if they don't get this thing going soon.

BARRY: You don't like it here?

CLIVE: I hate it. There's a kind of open air claustrophobia about this place.

AYESHA: It's called agoraphobia, Clive.

CLIVE: Yes yes, yes. That's not what I meant. I meant… Oh, I don't know, I just want to get away from here.

BARRY: Could be worse.

CLIVE: Could it?

BARRY: You're a white man in Israel. Not a black in South Africa. Not a Somali in Mogadishu. Not a Muslim in Bosnia. Not a Marsh Arab or a Kurd in Iraq.

AYESHA: I was in Baghdad just before the Gulf war.

BARRY: Spying were you?

AYESHA: No, not quite. I was working at the museum out there.

CLIVE: Reckons she saw Saddam Hussein.

AYESHA: I'm convinced it was him.

(*MAHMOUD looks up from his map to face CLIVE – CLIVE has a Saddam moustache that wasn't there before. MAHMOUD stares at him.*)

BARRY: Or one of him.

AYESHA: 'One of him'?

BARRY: It's a well known fact that Saddam uses several doubles.

(*FRAN looks up from the engine – she has a Saddam moustache. MAHMOUD stares at her.*)

AYESHA: Is it?

BARRY: Common knowledge.

(*DEIRDRE puts her head out of the mini-bus window – she has a Saddam moustache. MAHMOUD stares at her.*)

AYESHA: So you think it probably wasn't him...

(*MAHMOUD turns back to AYESHA and BARRY – they each have a Saddam moustache.*)

BARRY: You never know, you might have seen the real one.

(*MICHAEL re-enters – he has a Saddam moustache. MAHMOUD stares at him then covers his eyes for a moment. BARRY, AYESHA, CLIVE, DEIRDRE, MICHAEL and FRAN all remove their moustaches. MAHMOUD removes his hands from his eyes. He looks around – everything is as normal. MAHMOUD laughs to himself. DEIRDRE gets out of the bus, she is carrying a folding stool.*)

DEIRDRE: What are you laughing at?

MAHMOUD: Nothing. Just something I was imagining.

DEIRDRE: Really... Well, when you've got a minute perhaps you could imagine a way for us to get out of here. (*Tugging at a canopy fixed to the roof of the bus.*) How do you get this thing down? I can't sit in there it's like a bloody oven. (*MAHMOUD pulls the canopy down. DEIRDRE opens out her folding stool and sits down in the shade.*)

DEIRDRE: (*To MICHAEL.*) You came back, then.

MICHAEL: No darling, I'm a mirage. (*To MAHMOUD – referring to FRAN.*) Called out the emergency services, I see… Isn't that meant to be your job?

(*MAHMOUD ignores MICHAEL.*)

(*To FRAN.*) Little grease monkey, eh… Do a lot of this sort of thing, do you? Let me know if you need someone to hold your socket spanner for you.

FRAN: Piss off!

MICHAEL: Now, now… (*To MAHMOUD.*) Where are we?

(*MAHMOUD points out a coordinate on the map.*)

(*Pointing to a map reference.*) Is this where we were diverted from the main road?

MAHMOUD: Yes.

AYESHA: And you still have no idea why there was a diversion?

CLIVE: Or what happened to the signs?

MAHMOUD: I think there was some trouble.

MICHAEL: What sort of trouble?

MAHMOUD: A demonstration.

MICHAEL: Palestinians?

MAHMOUD: I don't know. I think so. A protest.

MICHAEL: Why the hell didn't you say before?

MAHMOUD: It's only a guess… I'm going to see what's up ahead. You should stay near the mini-bus.

MICHAEL: What's that supposed to mean?

MAHMOUD: There are snakes, perhaps scorpions…maybe even wolves.

CLIVE: Oh God.

MICHAEL: Listen, I suffer from a serious digestive disorder. My metabolism has to be regulated. I eat at specific times, one of those times is 1pm. Not five to, not five past, 1pm. We were supposed to have arrived in Jerusalem at 12.30 – it is now (*Glances at his watch.*) 12:33 precisely. There is nothing to eat here. I suggest you do something about it now.

MAHMOUD: Like what?

BARRY: I've got some peanuts.

MICHAEL: I don't want your bloody peanuts.

DEIRDRE: What about the people you radioed?

MAHMOUD: There'll be someone here soon.

DEIRDRE: There'd better be.

MICHAEL: You radioed your office?

MAHMOUD: Yes.

MICHAEL: That's a start, I suppose.

CLIVE: Why don't you wait here?

MAHMOUD: I won't be long.

FRAN: What about getting this thing started?

MAHMOUD: Can you do it?

FRAN: Don't know. Do you want me to keep trying?

MAHMOUD: Yes. That would be best.

> (*MAHMOUD exits stage right.*)

DEIRDRE: Marvellous. Here we are, stuck in the middle of nowhere, and our driver pisses off on walkabout.

> (*DEIRDRE gets onto the bus.*)

CLIVE: He better hurry up – I'm not exactly ecstatic about being left here.

AYESHA: Relax.

CLIVE: How?

AYESHA: Clive, you spent all day yesterday and the day before stretched out on a beach –

CLIVE: It's not the same here, and you know it.

AYESHA: I can't help it if you're frightened of snakes.

CLIVE: Don't! Just don't even talk about it.

AYESHA: You should have done what that woman said and kept forcing yourself to face up to your fear.

CLIVE: You don't exactly get a lot of snakes in West Hampstead.

AYESHA: There is such a thing as London Zoo, Clive – just.

BARRY: You don't want to worry yourself about a few snakes and insects.

CLIVE: Oh no, if they don't get us the wolves will.

BARRY: They won't come near us, they're frightened of human beings.

> (*BARRY gets back onto the bus.*)

CLIVE: That why you're hiding, is it?

> (*The PALESTINIAN seen at the start of the play cycles on.*)

FRAN: Hey… You… You, come here.

MICHAEL: Shut up for Christ's sake!

FRAN: Stop!

(MICHAEL grabs FRAN's arm.)

(To MICHAEL.) Get off!

(The PALESTINIAN stops. DEIRDRE gets out of the bus – she is smoking a cigarette.)

(To PALESTINIAN.) Can you get help? Broken do… *(Slowly.)* H-e-l-p…

(BARRY gets out of the bus – he is rolling a joint. The PALESTINIAN stares at them. He takes a lingering look at the mini-bus, then turns his bike and exits the way he came.)

MICHAEL: You bloody idiot!

FRAN: Eh?

MICHAEL: Do you have any idea who I am?

FRAN: No.

MICHAEL: I am Michael Leach, President of the First National Melbourne Bank.

FRAN: And I'm Fran Stott. Pleased to meet you.

MICHAEL: Jesus! Ask yourself where we we are… For crying out loud, woman – this is the West Bank. Do you want to be a hostage? Because I certainly don't. Christ, he could be Hizbollah, Hamas –

CLIVE: Oh my God, we're going to be kidnapped! Or murdered. Here. Now.

AYESHA: Don't be ridiculous.

MICHAEL: You saw him staring at the number plates – Israeli number plates. Christ knows who he's going to tell about us. You saw him snooping about earlier.

FRAN: You're not Jewish, are you?

MICHAEL: Of course I'm not bloody Jewish! Do you honestly think they're going to take that into consideration?

FRAN: He looked alright to me.

MICHAEL: He's Palestinian – As far as those people are concerned these are the occupied territories.

CLIVE: No, that's all changed now.

MICHAEL: This isn't Jericho. This isn't Gaza. It's not as if grudging recognition and some kind of token self-rule has suddenly turned all these Islamic types into saints overnight.

AYESHA: You're an authority on this, are you?

MICHAEL: All it's achieved is to make the extremists more extreme. Do you really think they're going to take kindly to a bus load of tourists?

(*MICHAEL climbs up onto the roof of the bus and stares out through his binoculars.*)

CLIVE: How long do you think the driver will be gone?

AYESHA: No idea. Don't worry, Clive. We'll be alright.

BARRY: Think positive. We'll get to Jerusalem.

MICHAEL: (*To BARRY.*) I hope that's not what I think it is.

BARRY: It's exactly what you think it is, and you can't have any.

MICHAEL: How dare you insinuate that I would smoke that stuff.

DEIRDRE: He smokes it all the time at home.

MICHAEL: (*Indignant.*) No I do not!

(*BARRY sits, he lights the joint and starts scribbling in a note book.*)

That Palestinian boy seems to have disappeared into thin air. And no sign of our Mr Said, either.

(*MICHAEL climbs down and rejoins the others.*)

Now all we have to do is wait for Islamic Jihad to come and chain us to a hot water pipe for the next five years.

AYESHA: Not every Muslim is a terrorist.

MICHAEL: No, but it helps.

AYESHA: You are beginning to get on my nerves.

CLIVE: Forget it, Ayesha.

(*BARRY stands and reads from his notebook.*)

BARRY: The Sun beats
The Sun bakes
The World turns
The World takes
My heart bleeds
My heart breaks

MICHAEL: That's appalling.

CLIVE: Who wrote it?

BARRY: I did.

(*MICHAEL moves upstage.*)

AYESHA: You're a poet?

BARRY: Apparently not.

MICHAEL: There's a cave back here.

(*BARRY crosses to MICHAEL.*)

AYESHA: (*Facetiously.*) Probably a Hamas ammunition dump.
(*BARRY takes a look inside the cave, then crosses to the bus and pulls out a ruck sack.*)

CLIVE: What are you doing?
(*BARRY takes a torch from the rucksack.*)

BARRY: Take a look inside.
(*BARRY crosses to the cave.*)

CLIVE: Are you mad! It could be full of snakes and all kind of things.

FRAN: If you're not out by the time I get this thing started we're going without you.
(*Islamic / Moorish music. Lights down.*)

Two

As before – half an hour later. DEIRDRE is reading a magazine. FRAN is sitting by the engine playing her recorder. MICHAEL is staring offstage. CLIVE is sitting on the footplate of the bus, AYESHA is standing beside him holding a copy of a short medieval play entitled The Play of Saint George *– she is testing CLIVE on his lines.*

CLIVE: Again.

AYESHA: Do I have to?

CLIVE: Yes. Give me my cue – 'What can you cure?'. About half way down the page.

AYESHA: I know where it is Clive, I've done it enough times. (*Reading from the script.*) What can you cure?

CLIVE: (*Reciting the Doctor's lines from* The Play of Saint George.)

All sorts of diseases,

Whatever you pleases –

DEIRDRE: What is that crap?

CLIVE: Do you mind, I'm trying to concentrate.

DEIRDRE: Sounds bloody stupid to me.

CLIVE: It's a precursor of the medieval trope.

DEIRDRE: The what?

CLIVE: Trope. Oh forget it. (*To AYESHA.*) Where was I?

AYESHA: Whatever you pleases –

CLIVE: (*Reciting lines.*) The phthisic, the palsy, and the gout.

Whatever the disorder, I soon draw it out.

AYESHA: (*Reading from the script.*) What is your fee?

CLIVE: (*Reciting lines.*) Fifteen pounds is all my fee –

DEIRDRE: Trope, you say. How do you spell that?

CLIVE: You're doing this deliberately.

DEIRDRE: No.

MICHAEL: (*Looking offstage.*) This is ridiculous. Where the hell's he got to?

CLIVE: Listen here. I'm trying to learn my lines. I open in this play in London in three weeks –

AYESHA: It's only five minutes outside a church in Hornsey, Clive.

CLIVE: That's not the point, Now, if you'll kindly allow me to continue. (*Reciting lines.*)

Fifteen pounds is all my fee,
The money you lay down.
But since 'tis such a rogue as he,
I'll cure him for ten pounds.
(*MAHMOUD enters. FRAN stops playing.*)

DEIRDRE: (*To MAHMOUD.*) Welcome back.

MICHAEL: Where have you been?

MAHMOUD: I've been considering what we should do.

MICHAEL: And?

MAHMOUD: I think we should stay here with the mini-bus.

MICHAEL: Brilliant! Well, while you were away concluding that we should do nothing we had a visitor.

MAHMOUD: Visitor?

MICHAEL: That Palestinian boy. The one on the bicycle who was hanging about when we got here. (*Pointing to FRAN.*) This idiot took it upon herself to stop him and ask for help.

MAHMOUD: (*To FRAN.*) Good. Good.

MICHAEL: Good! He could be on his way up here with an armed militia this very moment. Well? Couldn't he? Tell me I'm wrong, if I'm wrong. Christ knows, for once in my life I'd like to be.

MAHMOUD: You're wrong.

MICHAEL: Rubbish… There's every chance he could belong to some kind of extremist Islamic group.

AYESHA: You're getting carried away.

MICHAEL: They don't all love Arafat, you know… (*To MAHMOUD.*) What do you intend to do about it?

MAHMOUD: What can I do?

CLIVE: (*To MAHMOUD.*) Are you certain there aren't terrorists up here?

MAHMOUD: Yes. (*To FRAN – indicating the mini-bus.*) No use?

FRAN: I know what the problem is, I just haven't quite worked out how to solve it yet.
(*FRAN starts working on the engine again.*)

AYESHA: Is there a village or anything nearby?

MAHMOUD: I don't think so.

CLIVE: There must be something.

MAHMOUD: I didn't want to go too far. Where's the other one?

AYESHA: In there (*She points to the cave.*) – somewhere.

MAHMOUD: I said not to go off.

DEIRDRE: Shouldn't the people you radioed be here by now?

MAHMOUD: They were very busy.

DEIRDRE: Oh, bloody marvellous.

MICHAEL: I don't believe this. I suggest you call them again.

MAHMOUD: It won't make them get here faster.

CLIVE: Ayesha... (*Reciting lines.*) I have a little bottle of
    Elucumpane... Ayesha...

AYESHA: Not now, Clive.

> (*CLIVE snatches the script from AYESHA and walks away from
> her.*)

CLIVE: (*Reciting lines to himself.*)
    Here Jack, take a little of this flip-flop,
    Pour it down thy tip-top,
    Then rise up and fight again.

MAHMOUD: (*To FRAN.*) What's this?

FRAN: I don't know. A play or something he's meant to be
    doing outside a church when he gets back.

> (*BARRY emerges from the cave.*)

MAHMOUD: I told you not to leave here.

> (*BARRY holds out five small bones.*)

BARRY: They're bones of some sort. Goes on for miles in there
    you know.

DEIRDRE: Bones.

MICHAEL: (*To MAHMOUD.*) Now tell me I'm talking rubbish.

MAHMOUD: There are wolves.

MICHAEL: How are we to know those aren't human remains?

MAHMOUD: No.

AYESHA: (*To BARRY.*) Can I have a look?

BARRY: Sure.

> (*BARRY hands the bones to AYESHA.*)

MICHAEL: What if someone removed those diversion signs
    deliberately? Once a vehicle left the main road it would be
    bound to get lost up here. Just think how many Jews and
    Christians they could murder on their way to Jerusalem.

AYESHA: (*To MAHMOUD.*) Ignore him. He doesn't know what
    he's talking about.

MICHAEL: I wouldn't expect a bloody Hindu to understand.

AYESHA: I'm not Hindu.

MICHAEL: You're Muslim?

AYESHA: Yes.

MICHAEL: Where's your head thing and all that?

AYESHA: I choose not to wear hijab.

MICHAEL: Christ, a Muslim, that's all we need.

CLIVE: That's enough of that.

MICHAEL: Not you, as well?

CLIVE: No. But what if I was? What difference would it make?

DEIRDRE: So which one of you two is going to convert? (*To CLIVE.*) I can't see you praying to Mecca five times a day.

CLIVE: I may not be the sort to start praying to Mecca, but I'll tell you something, there was a time when I was ready to pack my bags and go off to Bosnia to fight with the Muslims.

MICHAEL: You should have contacted me. I'm sure I could've arranged something for you.

FRAN: (*From behind bonnet.*) I wanted to go to Afghanistan.
(*FRAN emerges from behind the bonnet.*)

DEIRDRE: What the hell for?

FRAN: There was a time when I did a lot of reading about the Sufis. Shari'ah, Tariqah, Haqiqah and all that. Recognizing the road, travelling the road, and arriving at the city of knowledge.

DEIRDRE: Which is more than can be said for our achievements today.

FRAN: No. Don't take the piss. I felt an affinity with it.
(*FRAN once again ducks out of sight behind the bus to continue working on the engine.*)
(*From behind the bonnet.*) Yes. I was going to go to Afghanistan and fight with the Mujaheddin.

MICHAEL: Ridiculous.
(*MAHMOUD's imagination: FRAN leaps out from behind the bonnet dressed as an Afghan Mujaheddin fighter. She throws an hand-grenade and dives for cover back behind the bus. MAHMOUD throws open his arms and imitates the sound of an explosion, at the same time there is a huge explosion offstage – this explosion is in MAHMOUD's imagination and is not heard by anyone else, all they see are the gesticulations and sounds he makes.*)

MICHAEL: (*To MAHMOUD.*) What on earth are you doing?

MAHMOUD: My ally in the Holy war is throwing handgrenades at Soviet troops.

MICHAEL: The man is insane. We're in the hands of a lunatic and a whirling dervish.

DEIRDRE: So why didn't you go?

(*FRAN peers out – she is dressed as normal.*)

FRAN: I was too young. Couldn't afford it.

DEIRDRE: If you really want to do something you can always find a way.

MICHAEL: Amen.

FRAN: Like how?

DEIRDRE: You could've got media sponsorship.

FRAN: I'm not bloody Sandy Gall, you know.

DEIRDRE: Who?

FRAN: Anyway, I got fed up with it.

AYESHA: Fed up?

FRAN: Yes. It got a bit too…Islamic.

AYESHA: It's meant to be Islamic.

FRAN: I know. It just started to feel like I'd shaken off one male religious straightjacket for another.

AYESHA: But that's because it's what the men have done to it. The Prophet himself said: 'The true school is the Mother.'

FRAN: It just didn't feel right, that's all. And besides, it was about then I started to get into Buddhism.

(*FRAN continues working on the engine.*)

MICHAEL: (*To MAHMOUD.*) Do you have no idea what time your partners in crime might get here?

MAHMOUD: Who?

MICHAEL: The people you called.

MAHMOUD: We'll have to be patient.

MICHAEL: You are in a great deal of trouble.

DEIRDRE: If we'd flown like I suggested we'd never have got stuck in this mess in the first place.

FRAN: (*Frightened – under her breath.*) Mahmoud… Mahmoud… Mahmoud…

MAHMOUD: Yes…

FRAN: Down by my foot.

(*MAHMOUD slowly crosses to FRAN.*)

MAHMOUD: Right. Don't move.

FRAN: What is it?

MAHMOUD: An asp.

(*FRAN looks terrified. CLIVE looks terrified.*)

DEIRDRE: Shit! An asp… Here comes Cleopatra – Let's have a look.

(*DEIRDRE crosses to MAHMOUD. DEIRDRE pushes MAHMOUD to one side and crouches down.*)

Must be a young 'un. I've seen snakes bigger than that crossing the road in Guluguba. Shouldn't be a problem.

(*DEIRDRE takes a wrench from the tool box, she remains perfectly still for a moment, then pins the snake to the ground with the wrench.*)

Got him!

FRAN: Thank God for that.

DEIRDRE: Looks like a small cobra to me.

(*DEIRDRE holds up the snake.*)

There you go – what a beaut!

CLIVE: Oh my God!

DEIRDRE: What's wrong with you?

CLIVE: Snake… No… No…

DEIRDRE: Not frightened of it, are you? Look, you can get it to secrete its venom if you press it here.

CLIVE: Please…

DEIRDRE: Venom has medicinal uses, you know. Friend of mine's got a snake farm up in Queensland. You want to hold it?

CLIVE: NO!

AYESHA: Leave him alone.

DEIRDRE: Here you go, mate.

AYESHA: Get rid of it.

(*DEIRDRE pretends to drop the snake.*)

DEIRDRE: Oh no, dropped it.

(*CLIVE faints.*)

Bloody Poms,,,

(*DEIRDRE pins the snake down again with the wrench and looks around for a rock.*)

AYESHA: Clive… Clive…

(*AYESHA helps CLIVE to sit up.*)

FRAN: Is he alright?

AYESHA: He's got a phobia about snakes.

FRAN: I'm not that keen myself.

AYESHA: Clive, are you okay? Clive…

CLIVE: Yes. I'm fine… fine. Don't fuss, please. It's nothing.

(*DEIRDRE screams.*)

DEIRDRE: It bit me, it bit me! – I'm dying…

MICHAEL: Deirdre!

(*DEIRDRE grins.*)

DEIRDRE: Just kidding.

MICHAEL: Will I never learn.

(*DEIRDRE picks up a rock and brings it down on the snake's head several times.*)

DEIRDRE: There…Happy now?

CLIVE: My God, she's like something escaped from *Prisoner Cell Block H.*

BARRY: The snake? It would not rust on its forked tree. (*To MICHAEL.*) Derek Walcott. Before you say something you might regret.

FRAN: You ever heard of a Sufi poet called Rumi?

MICHAEL: Friend of yours, is he?

FRAN: Not exactly, he died about seven hundred years ago.

(*MAHMOUD's imagination: BARRY becomes Rumi – MAHMOUD recites the words with BARRY.*)

BARRY: (*As Rumi.*) Rise, and go where the friend is. Stay with the people who love that presence. There are traps to leap across and snares to circle around, but if the friend drives you from the door, climb up and sneak down over the roof.

MICHAEL: (*Pointing to MAHMOUD.*) Look, he's talking to himself now.

MAHMOUD: Jalal ad-Din Rumi.

(*AYESHA helps CLIVE to stand. CLIVE leans against the bus.*)

BARRY: (*To CLIVE.*) Man, you look as pale as a ghost.

CLIVE: I've always had this thing about snakes.

AYESHA: You should have seen the state of him when he had to play a snake charmer in *Aladdin* last year.

CLIVE: And they were rubber.

BARRY: You're an actor?

CLIVE: Yes.

BARRY: I thought you looked familiar.

(*CLIVE perks up.*)

CLIVE: Really.

BARRY: Now what is it I might have seen you in? You done much telly?

CLIVE: *The Bill.*

BARRY: No.

CLIVE: *Casualty.*

BARRY: No.

AYESHA: Russ Abbot.

CLIVE: Shut up!

BARRY: Russ Abbot… I like him.

CLIVE: I'm mainly a theatre actor.

BARRY: Ah, must have mistaken you for someone else then.

CLIVE: Probably.

BARRY: You got much work on at the moment?

BARRY: I'm playing the Doctor in a medieval piece called *The Play of Saint George.* Not much else on the horizon though, I have to admit.

BARRY: Times are hard.

CLIVE: Very hard. I can't really complain. I've just finished a run as Iago in *Othello.*

AYESHA: That was two years ago.

(*FRAN climbs up into the driver's seat of the bus. She turns the key in the ignition. The engine fires for a moment, then cuts. FRAN tries the ignition again, this time there is nothing. FRAN gets down from the bus.*)

FRAN: Better luck next time…

(*FRAN returns to the engine. AYESHA sits and inspects the bones given to her by BARRY.*)

MICHAEL: Deirdre, have you got my mobile phone?

MAHMOUD: You've got a phone?

DEIRDRE: I didn't bring it.

MICHAEL: I asked you to put it in your bag.

DEIRDRE: No you didn't.

MICHAEL: You stupid –

DEIRDRE: What? Go on, say it.

MICHAEL: Oh, it doesn't matter.

DEIRDRE: I didn't bring it because I thought it'd do you good to get away from the blasted phone.

MICHAEL: As insightful as ever.

DEIRDRE: This was your idea, don't forget.

MICHAEL: How could I bloody forget, you keep reminding me every five minutes. (*To MAHMOUD.*) Contact your office

on that radio, would you – I'd like them to fax Australia
for me.

MAHMOUD: No.

MICHAEL: What do you mean 'No'? It's your incompetence
that's got us stranded here. I think it's the least you can do.

MAHMOUD: The radio isn't working.

DEIRDRE: What about earlier –

MAHMOUD: It isn't working.

DEIRDRE: So there's no one coming?

MAHMOUD: I'm hoping that when we don't arrive someone
will be sent to look for us.

MICHAEL: Who? They don't even know we exist. The coach
left without us.

MAHMOUD: The office in Jerusalem know we are coming.

DEIRDRE: Who's going to find us up here?

MAHMOUD: There's nothing else I can do. Sorry.

MICHAEL: Sorry! You'll be bloody sorry, if you don't get this
damn relic going!

AYESHA: Mahmoud, can I have a word?

(*AYESHA takes MAHMOUD away from the others.*)

(*Holding up the bones given to her by BARRY.*) These aren't
animal bones.

MAHMOUD: No?

AYESHA: They're metacarpals. At least I think they are…From
a hand. Here… (*She lays one of the bones on the back of her
hand.*) Between the wrist and the fingers.

MAHMOUD: Those are human bones?

AYESHA: I'm pretty sure they're human. I've seen skeletons
before, when I've been on digs. Chances are they've been
lying in there for hundreds of years, but I can't be certain.

MAHMOUD: Don't tell them, please.

AYESHA: No.

(*CLIVE crosses to AYESHA and MAHMOUD.*)

CLIVE: What's going on?

(*MAHMOUD moves away.*)

AYESHA: Nothing.

(*AYESHA re-joins the others.*)

(*To BARRY.*) Do you know what these bones are?

BARRY: Don't tell me – The foot of Pontius Pilate.

AYESHA: Not exactly. They belong to some kind of rodent.

BARRY: No. Too big.

AYESHA: I'm not talking about a mouse or a squirrel. Some rodents can reach a length of over four feet, they can weigh as much as 75–100 lbs.

BARRY: What sort of rodent?

AYESHA: I'm not exactly sure. I've seen a lot of animal skeletons on archaeological digs, but never anything quite like this. They certainly don't belong to anything that died recently.

BARRY: An extinct species?

AYESHA: I'm not a palaeontologist.

MICHAEL: (*To AYESHA.*) Let me have a look.

(*AYESHA gives the bones to MICHAEL.*)

AYESHA: They were probably dug up by wolves.

BARRY: Time to do some excavating.

(*BARRY turns to go.*)

AYESHA: You shouldn't disturb anything –

(*BARRY disappears into the cave. MICHAEL hands the bones back to AYESHA and gets into the mini-bus.*)

DEIRDRE: (*To AYESHA.*) You go on a lot of archaeological digs, do you?

AYESHA: Last one was three years ago, just outside Arbil in Northern Iraq. Several of the things we found there will be in the exhibition in Jerusalem.

DEIRDRE: The ceramics you were talking about?

AYESHA: Not just ceramics.

DEIRDRE: Got anything I can look at?

AYESHA: Yes. In here…

(*AYESHA takes a book from her bag, she opens it and hands it to DEIRDRE.*)

Like this.

(*DEIRDRE turns over the page.*)

DEIRDRE: I like that.

(*AYESHA points out a picture to DEIRDRE.*)

AYESHA: This is one of my favourite pieces.

DEIRDRE: What is it?

AYESHA: It's a ewer – jug, a pitcher of some sort… It's bronze. Look… You see this square, elegant decoration – It's kufic inscription. Kufic scripts were used from earliest Islamic times in Korans. This dates from the eleventh or twelfth century. See… It's inlaid with silver.

FRAN: (*To MAHMOUD.*) Try it.

(*MAHMOUD gets into the bus and turns the key in the ignition. The engine turns over, but dies almost immediately. MAHMOUD tries again – the same thing happens. MICHAEL peers out from the bus. MAHMOUD tries a third time – the same thing happens. MAHMOUD gets out of the mini-bus.*)

FRAN: I suppose we could always try pushing it.

DEIRDRE: Problem… We got a flat tyre.

(*MICHAEL gets out of the bus. CLIVE sits on the floor.*)

MAHMOUD: There's a spare, I can change it.

(*MICHAEL moves away from the bus to once again survey the area through his binoculars. MAHMOUD removes a spare from the rear of the bus and begins to change the tyre. AYESHA puts away the book she has been showing DEIRDRE and crosses to CLIVE.*)

CLIVE: What did I tell you. It's just like that film. It's sabotage I tell you… (*To MAHMOUD.*) I don't suppose you remember who played the German spy in *Ice-Cold in Alex*?

(*MAHMOUD shakes his head. AYESHA puts an arm around CLIVE.*)

Get off!

AYESHA: What's got into you?

CLIVE: I want to get out of here.

AYESHA: We all do.

(*AYESHA goes to touch CLIVE again. He pushes her away.*)

Clive!

CLIVE: I'm sick and tired of all this. I knew I should've stayed in London.

AYESHA: Let's go through your lines.

CLIVE: No.

AYESHA: It's a bus. It's broken down. It's not a conspiracy, Clive.

CLIVE: I wouldn't expect you to understand.

AYESHA: I never do, do I.

CLIVE: Go on, say it – Get a proper job, Clive. Give up acting.

AYESHA: When have I ever said that to you?

CLIVE: You imply it.

AYESHA: Don't be stupid… And don't sulk.

CLIVE: Right! That's it! I've had it! It's over. Everything's over. I'm giving everything up. Acting, eating, drinking, walking, sleeping – Everything. No more plays. No more coffee. No tea. A complete alcohol ban. Mineral water only – Aqua Libra, maybe. No – just water. Salads. No meat. Regular, healthy exercise. No, no exercise, I shall become totally inert. No newspapers. No books – Not even Shakespeare. And definitely no television. I shall abstain from everything. I'll never act, eat, drink, sleep nor think again, and I shall remain celebate until the day I die.

AYESHA: You won't last twenty-four hours.

CLIVE: Ha! That's what you think.

AYESHA: You know, according to the Council of Nablus in 1120, any Christian man who kept a Muslim woman as a concubine was to be castrated and have his nose cut off.

CLIVE: Lucky I'm an atheist then, isn't it.

AYESHA: I still say you won't last twenty-four hours.

CLIVE: You know, you can be very dull sometimes.

AYESHA: There's no need for that, Clive.

CLIVE: (*Mimicking AYESHA.*) 'According to the council of… wherever-it-was…'

AYESHA: I'm sorry if I bore you, Clive. Tell you what, if you find my company so uninspiring, perhaps the next time you're 'resting' you can arrange to get your alms from someone else.

CLIVE: There you are – Get a proper job or get out.

AYESHA: Well what do you expect. I'm fed up of you sitting around at home bemoaning the parts you never get and playing bloody Super Mario on my computer.
(*MICHAEL gets onto the bus.*)

CLIVE: That's below the belt, Ayesha.

AYESHA: It had to be said.
(*CLIVE crosses to MAHMOUD and begins to help him change the wheel. MAHMOUD leans inside the mini-bus.*)

MAHMOUD: (*To MICHAEL.*) Excuse me, can you get out of the bus, please. We have to change the tyre.

DEIRDRE: (*Bangs on side of bus.*) Michael!

MICHAEL: (*Shouting from inside the mini-bus.*) Ouch! Shit!

DEIRDRE: Now what?
(*MICHAEL limps out of the bus.*)

MICHAEL: I've banged my blasted knee.

DEIRDRE: Quick – Call the flying doctor.

MICHAEL: Thank you for your sympathy.

DEIRDRE: You're insured, aren't you.

MICHAEL: Very funny.

(*AYESHA crosses to CLIVE.*)

AYESHA: Sorry.

CLIVE: Forget it.

AYESHA: Clive –

CLIVE: No. You're right. You're absolutely right. Apart from one thing… It's Sonic the Hedgehog, not Super Mario… Anyway, it's my fault, I shouldn't have started –

MICHAEL: Look at that.

DEIRDRE: What?

MICHAEL: If I'm not very much mistaken, there are a brace of quail over there.

CLIVE: Quail! That's it!

MICHAEL: *Coturnix coturnix.* Old world game birds.

CLIVE: Anthony Quayle.

MICHAEL: I beg your pardon?

CLIVE: Anthony Quayle played the German spy in *Ice-Cold in Alex.* Ayesha –

AYESHA: I heard.

MICHAEL: He's off his head. Is everyone going mad around here, or am I just imagining it?

AYESHA: He's not as bad as some people.

MICHAEL: What was that?

AYESHA: I was just thinking, if you're really lucky perhaps you might see Sinbad transported from the Valley of Diamonds in the claws of the giant roc.

MICHAEL: What on earth are you talking about, woman?

AYESHA: The great white bird of Arabian legend. Haven't you read the *Arabian Nights*?

MICHAEL: No.

CLIVE: You must've seen the film.

MICHAEL: No, I haven't.

(*A huge shadow crosses the stage. MAHMOUD watches it as it passes overhead.*)

What are you staring at? (*He follows MAHMOUD's gaze up to the sky.*) It's a cloud.

(The shaddow passes and bright light returns.)

DEIRDRE: *(To AYESHA.)* Hey… Show him the picture of that jug.

MICHAEL: Jug?

DEIRDRE: Thing she found.

AYESHA: I didn't exactly find it.

MICHAEL: We collect antiques and fine art, you know. We have a Modigliani.

AYESHA: Yes, I know.

MICHAEL: And a Constable. Worth a fortune.

(DEIRDRE takes AYESHA's book.)

AYESHA: Do you mind?

(AYESHA goes to take the book back, but DEIRDRE pulls it away from her and passes it to MICHAEL.)

Give it to me.

MICHAEL: What page?

AYESHA: Give me the book.

MICHAEL: I can find it. Just tell me what page.

AYESHA: Will you kindly return –

MICHAEL: My brother's the man you should see about selling this sort of stuff.

AYESHA: Those are museum pieces. They're not for sale.

MICHAEL: Everything his its price, dear.

AYESHA: Don't you dare call me 'dear'!

MICHAEL: Sorry, love. Mind you, Philip's collection leans more towards the military – helmets, insignia, cannon, that kind of thing.

AYESHA: Give it back!

MICHAEL: *(Still withholding the book.)* He's in the army, see. Colonel. Saw action in the Falklands. And the Gulf. Had to clear up that damn mess after the Iraqis lost their nerve and pulled out of Kuwait. Carnage.

(FRAN climbs into the drivers seat of the bus.)

Wreckage strewn for miles. Must've been like shooting fish in a barrel. A turkey shoot one of the pilots called it… Are you feeling alright? Haven't upset you, have I?

AYESHA: They weren't fish, they weren't turkeys, they were human beings, and they were shot in the back after Iraq had agreed to an unconditional withdrawl.

MICHAEL: So you condone Saddam's actions, do you?

AYESHA: They were murdered.

(*FRAN turns the key in the ignition. The bus starts up.*)

MAHMOUD: You're a genius.

FRAN: I know.

MAHMOUD: It started. I can't believe it.

FRAN: Don't know how long for though.

(*FRAN revs the engine.*)

MICHAEL: Come on, let's get out of this God-forsaken place.

(*MICHAEL hands the book to AYESHA.*)

(*To MAHMOUD.*) Come on you, hurry, hurry. Might even make it in time for a late lunch.

DEIRDRE: What about… What's that bloke's name?

AYESHA: Barry.

MICHAEL: Get that wheel changed and we'll be out of here quicker than in Iraqi out of Kuwait!

(*MAHMOUD's imagination: sudden sound of aeroplanes, explosions, fire. Sudden cut back to normal. Silence – the engine has cut. FRAN gets out of the bus and looks at the engine. She then looks in the fuel tank.*)

FRAN: (*To MAHMOUD.*) Your fuel gauge is broken – We're out of diesel.

MICHAEL: (*To MAHMOUD.*) I'll sue you and your tin-pot company all the way to hell for this.

(*The PALESTINIAN cycles on and stops. For a moment no one moves, then MAHMOUD crosses to him and they have a discreet conversation. The cyclist unstraps a large suitcase from the rear of his bike and places it on the ground. MAHMOUD gives the cyclist some money. The cyclist takes out a gun and hands it to MAHMOUD. Everyone freezes. BARRY re-emerges from the cave holding a human skull.*)

BARRY: Look what I found.

(*Islamic / Moorish music. Lights down.*)

Three

As at the end of the previous scene. No time has elapsed. The cyclist gets back on his bike and exits. MAHMOUD is holding the gun.

MAHMOUD: Don't panic, I'm not going to shoot anyone. It's to frighten the wolves away.
(*MAHMOUD puts the gun under the driver's seat.*)
He's brought us some food and something to drink. I've given him some money. He'll be back with a tow truck later. In the meantime I suggest we eat. It's half past one, Mr Leach, I hope that's not too late for you.

DEIRDRE: Why didn't you just tell him to get some petrol?

FRAN: Diesel. It's not that simple. You can't just fill it up again, you have to bleed the injectors and pump all the air out of the system. It could take ages.

MICHAEL: (*To MAHMOUD.*) You idiot!

MAHMOUD: I'll be able to sort out alternative transport for you as soon as we get down from here.

MICHAEL: Don't think you're getting away with this. (*To AYESHA.*) And you! A rodent you said. (*Indicating the skull.*) Explain that! Explain that! Doesn't look much like a rat, does it.

AYESHA: We all get things wrong.
(*AYESHA crosses to BARRY. She inspects the skull while BARRY holds it.*)

DEIRDRE: Michael, calm down. So Bob Marley dug up an old mate of his. Islamic Jihad turned out to be a Palestinian take-away. Paranoia over.

AYESHA: Listen, I knew the bones were human. But I'm convinced they don't belong to anyone who died recently. You can tell by the discolouration and progressive decay. I didn't want to alarm anyone.

DEIRDRE: There.

MICHAEL: Well I'm glad you believe her.
(*MAHMOUD opens the case. He takes out some fruit and water.*)

MAHMOUD: This is very generous.

MICHAEL: Half a dozen oranges and a bottle of water. A veritable feast.

MAHMOUD: He didn't have to bring us anything.

FRAN: There's plenty here. Goat's cheese, bread, biscuits.
(*FRAN, AYESHA, DEIRDRE, BARRY and MAHMOUD start to eat and drink. CLIVE picks at the food.*)

DEIRDRE: (*To MICHAEL.*) Sit down and eat something.
(*MICHAEL ignores her.*)

BARRY: (*To the skull.*) You want a drink? You look a bit thirsty to me.

AYESHA: Can I have a closer look?

BARRY: (*To the skull.*) What you think? (*He holds the skull up to his ear as if it's whispering to him.*) He says it's okay.
(*BARRY hands the skull to AYESHA.*)

FRAN: I knew it was a good idea to stop him.

MICHAEL: You'll change your tune if this turns out to be our last supper.

DEIRDRE: Ignore him, he's not well.

MICHAEL: I am in perfectly good health.

BARRY: How old you think it is?

AYESHA: It's very difficult to say. It's interesting though. Hermits would have lived in these mountains after their expulsion from the walls of Jerusalem in 1187. It was Saladin's capture of Jerusalem that year that precipitated the Third Crusade.

BARRY: He's eight hundred years old?

AYESHA: It's only a wild guess.

MICHAEL: Come on, Deirdre, we're getting out of here.

DEIRDRE: How?

MICHAEL: You can walk can't you.

DEIRDRE: I'm not walking anywhere.

MICHAEL: Give me some of that bread and cheese and I'll be on my way.

DEIRDRE: In your condition. Come off it, Michael, you won't get twenty yards.

MAHMOUD: It would be foolish for you to go.

AYESHA: Please, let him.

BARRY: Remember what happened to Robert Maxwell.

MICHAEL: I beg your pardon?

BARRY: Did he jump or was he pushed? They could be asking the same question about you when they find your body on the side of the road tomorrow.

MAHMOUD: Sit down and eat. It won't kill you to wait a short while longer and eat with us.

MICHAEL: How do you know it won't kill me? That food could be poisoned. Have any of you thought of that?

MAHMOUD: It's not poisoned.

MICHAEL: How do you know?

MAHMOUD: Why would he want to poison us?

MICHAEL: Because it's easier than taking us on hand to hand.

BARRY: He had a gun.

MICHAEL: That's just in case something goes wrong. This way all he has to do is wait half an hour, come back, and then take whatever he wants from us as we lay here dying or drugged up to the eyeballs. Come to think of it, this whole thing could be a set-up. How are we to know, for instance, that you (*Indicates MAHMOUD.*) aren't in on it? That this isn't something you two planned between you? Get us up here, drug us, rob us, then use the gun to finish off.

MAHMOUD: How did you guess.

MICHAEL: (*Taking the skull from AYESHA.*) How are we to know we won't end up like this?

MAHMOUD: I did not plan this. The food is not poisoned, I have no desire to rob you or to shoot you. Now, why don't you be quiet and give us all a moment's peace –

MICHAEL: Fact is, life is cheap here. These people would kill their Grandmother for the price of a Mercedes.

MAHMOUD: How can you say such things!

MICHAEL: Easily.

(*MICHAEL turns to go.*)

DEIRDRE: Michael, where are you going?

MICHAEL: For a slash.

(*MICHAEL crosses to the cave.*)

BARRY: Hey man, not in there, that's a sight of great archaeological interest.

(*MICHAEL goes into the cave.*)

The man has no respect.

FRAN: This tastes wonderful.

BARRY: Needs some Special Brew to wash it down.

CLIVE: (*To MAHMOUD.*) So there are wolves up here?

MAHMOUD: Yes. But I don't think they'll trouble us.

AYESHA: (*To CLIVE.*) Aren't you hungry?

CLIVE: The heat's made me lose my appetite. Perhaps we
could do something to occupy ourselves while we wait.

DEIRDRE: Like what?

CLIVE: A game.

DEIRDRE: A game? What, like the Olympics? Oh sorry, I
forgot you Brits don't like talking about the Olympics since
Sydney won the games.

AYESHA: Clive, I'm sure we're capable of passing the next
hour or so without having to resort to games.

CLIVE: I need something to occupy my mind.

DEIRDRE: You mean, you've actually got a mind to occupy?

AYESHA: Just relax, Clive.

CLIVE: I can't. I'm going to go through my lines for the play.
Ayesha –

AYESHA: Do I have to?

MAHMOUD: Can I?

CLIVE: Why don't we all do it? We could have a proper
reading. There are enough parts for everyone…
(*AYESHA, DEIRDRE and BARRY look disdainfully at CLIVE.*)
Fair enough. (*To MAHMOUD.*) Are you sure?

MAHMOUD: Of course. I read a lot of plays when I studied
English. I'd like to do it.
(*MICHAEL re-enters from the cave. He sits and eats.*)

CLIVE: Great. Thanks, Mahmoud.
(*CLIVE takes out his script and passes it to MAHMOUD, pointing
out the relevant section.*)

MAHMOUD: (*Reading.*) In the midst of much singing, dancing
and feasting –

DEIRDRE: When's the singing and dancing start?

CLIVE: Ignore that bit. Here, you do the Turkish Knight.

MAHMOUD: (*Reading.*) Open the doors and let me in!
I hope your favours now to win:
Whether I rise, or whether I fall,
I'll do my best to please you all.

CLIVE: And so on and so on. Enter Saint George, I'll do Saint
George. (*Reading.*)
Here come I, Saint George, from Britain I have sprung,
I'll fight the dragon bold, for my wonders have begun:
I'll clip his wings, he shall not fly;
I'll cut him down, or else I'll die.

DEIRDRE: Very good.

CLIVE: Shutup. Enter the Dragon.

DEIRDRE: I thought that was a film.

CLIVE: Will you please be quiet. (*To MAHMOUD.*) Here, my bit
    – Enter a Doctor.

MAHMOUD: (*Reading.*) What can you cure?

CLIVE: (*Reciting.*) All sorts of diseases,
    Whatever you pleases,
    The phthisic, the palsy, and the gout,
    Whatever the disorder, I soon draw it out.
    (*CLIVE and MAHMOUD continue going through the script in the
    background. BARRY lights up a spliff.*)

MICHAEL: I've warned you about that.

BARRY: Man, it's just a little rasta aperitif, that's all.

MICHAEL: Aperitif! You've already eaten twice as much as
    anyone else.

DEIRDRE: Can I have a smoke?
    (*BARRY passes the spliff to DEIRDRE.*)

MICHAEL: Deirdre. Don't you dare! Think about my
    reputation.

DEIRDRE: Oh, you're reputation's really going to be ruined
    when this lot see your wife smoking a joint half way up a
    mountain in the Israeli outback.

MICHAEL: Any one of these people could sell this story to the
    press. You won't be joking about it then.
    (*DEIRDRE draws on the spliff. FRAN starts to play the
    recorder.*)
    (*To FRAN.*) Do we have to?
    (*DEIRDRE passes the spliff back to BARRY.*)

DEIRDRE: Thanks, mate.
    (*DEIRDRE offers BARRY her hip flask.*)

BARRY: What is it?

DEIRDRE: Rum.

BARRY: Rum! I'm starting to like you. (*BARRY takes a drink.*)
    This is turning out to be a fine day. A red snapper and I'd
    be very contented. Hey, I got it, If you could have the best
    meal of your whole life right here, right now, what would
    it be?

MICHAEL: The meal of a condemned man, you mean.

DEIRDRE: Take no notice.

BARRY: You can choose anything.

MICHAEL: Sheeps' eyes.

AYESHA: You are so bloody arrogant.

MICHAEL: I've always found arrogance preferable to ignorance.

AYESHA: To which I would like to add – bigoted.

MICHAEL: It is not my problem if you feel inferior.

AYESHA: Inferior? What are you talking about?

(*CLIVE and MAHMOUD are distracted from the script by the argument.*)

MICHAEL: Civilization… Culture.

AYESHA: There are many legacies the West owes to Islam.

MICHAEL: Like Yugoslavia.

AYESHA: How dare you suggest that what's happening in Bosnia is the fault of the Muslims.

DEIRDRE: None of them are angels.

MICHAEL: Croats and Serbs have suffered just as much as your lot.

AYESHA: I know that. I'm not trying to invent a hierarchy of suffering.

MICHAEL: (*To FRAN.*) Did you know that under Islamic law you could have your hands chopped off for playing music that displeases the ruling elite.

AYESHA: Rubbish!

(*FRAN stops playing the recorder.*)

MICHAEL: Ah, sweet peace.

CLIVE: (*To MAHMOUD.*) Shall we…

(*CLIVE and MAHMOUD begin to go through the script again.*)

AYESHA: What about mathematics, science, learning… All things the West took from great Arab academics.

MICHAEL: What about them – Ideas taken from the Greeks, developed by the Arabs and conquered by the West. Now then, anything else you'd like to get off your chest?

AYESHA: Yes. Your attitude to art disgusts me.

MICHAEL: Meaning what, precisely?

AYESHA: The way you treat it as a commodity.

MICHAEL: Great art only exists because wealthy individuals are willing to pay a great deal of money for it. It's always been that way. I think you'll find through history that the wealthy nations were the cultured ones.

AYESHA: You know nothing about culture.

MICHAEL: I have collected art for over twenty years, I am a patron of both the National Gallery of Australia and the Australian Institute of Craft and Design. I may not be an authority on Islamic pots, but there is very little about fine art and architecture I do not know.

AYESHA: About Western art and architecture.

MICHAEL: Great art and architecture.

(*During the following section the lighting slate gradually alters as MAHMOUD's imagination slowly transforms the scene before him into twelfth-century Palestine at the time of the third crusade (1187 – 92). In order to do this a canopy is pulled down over the mini-bus so that it becomes a tent and each of the characters dress each other, item by item, in twelfth-century costume – MICHAEL becomes Richard I; DEIRDRE becomes Berengaria, Richard's wife; FRAN becomes Joan, Richard's sister; CLIVE becomes a Doctor; BARRY becomes a Moorish Trader; AYESHA becomes a Pregnant Muslim; MAHMOUD becomes Saladin. The twelfth-century costumes should consist of basic items that can be worn over existing present day costume, it is not neccessary to cover entirely the present day costume as anachronistic elements of dress are desirable. Further anachronisms should be added – an armalite for MICHAEL; a blue UN beret for DEIRDRE; a Gucci bag for FRAN; a portable phone for BARRY; an American baseball cap for AYESHA; a syringe for CLIVE; a gun belt for MAHMOUD. At the same time the upstage rock face transfigures into the facade of a church in the same style as the buildings carved out of the red sandstone cliffs at Petra. CLIVE and MAHMOUD continue to go through* The Play of Saint George.)

AYESHA: Can't you appreciate a piece of art for what it is, rather than what it costs, where it came from, or who made it?

MICHAEL: I appreciate well-made art, not a collection of indecipherable scribbles.

AYESHA: By 'indecipherable scribbles' I take it you mean Arabic calligraphy, geometric design, arabesque ornament –

MICHAEL: Call it what you like, I've seen more innovative design in Woolworths. No, nothing can match the tradition of art in the West.

AYESHA: Islamic art has an equally fine tradition.

MICHAEL: I don't think so. Nothing compares to the sculpture –

AYESHA: Mosaics, metalwork, ceramics –

MICHAEL: Painting. The art of the renaissance – Piero della Francesca.

AYESHA: The Mughal school. Fifteenth century Persian art – The paintings of Bihzad.

MICHAEL: Engraving.

AYESHA: Safavid brocades; the Ardebil carpet; woven silks.

MICHAEL: Architecture – Buckingham Palace; Sydney Opera House.

AYESHA: Architecture – The Alhambra; Taj Mahal.

MICHAEL: Westminster Abbey; Notre Dame.

AYESHA: The Mosque of Sultan Ahmed; the Great Mosque at Cordova.

MICHAEL: The Tower of London; Windsor, Warwick –

AYESHA: Fortifications – The Bab el-Futuh, Cairo. Many features of which were taken to the West by the Crusaders.

MICHAEL: The Crusades. The art of war taught to the infidel by the great powers of Europe.

AYESHA: Art! The First Crusade – For eighteen hours after the fall of Jerusalem the Christian army ran riot, slaughtering ordinary Muslims and Jews. The Children's Crusade – Thousands of children killed or sold into slavery. The Third Crusade – Richard the First –

MICHAEL: Ah – Good king Richard. Richard Coeur de Lion. Richard the Lionheart.

AYESHA: 1189. The Third Crusade. 'Good' King Richard voyages to the Holy Land. To join crusading armies before the walls of Acre, and take command of this siege with his 'chivalrous' hand.

(*The dressing of characters in the anachronistic costume of the twelfth century / Third Crusade, and the transfiguration of the bus into a tent and the rock face into the façade of a church should now be complete. The next section of the play is loosely based on an early pagan drama assimilated by medieval Christians called* The Play of Saint George. *This version of the play segues in with the text as recited by CLIVE and MAHMOUD.*)

MICHAEL: (*As Richard I.*)

Here come I, Richard Cœur de Lion,
Welcome, or welcome not.
I know Richard the Lionheart
Will never be forgot.
I have not come here to laugh or to jeer,
But for a pocketful of money and a skinful of beer
To show some sport or passtime
Gentlemen and Ladies, in the Crusades time.
If you will not believe what I now say,
Come in the Muslim warrior, Saladin! Clear the way.
(*MAHMOUD (as Saladin) moves forward.*)

MAHMOUD: (*As Saladin.*)

Here come I, Saladin, sultan of Egypt,
Welcome, or welcome not.
I know the saracen Saladin
Will never be forgot.
King Richard stands beyond, but swears he'll force in
To the city of Acre, and pierce infidel skin.
If you do not believe what I now say,
Come in Richard's Queen – Clear the way.
(*DEIRDRE (as Berengaria) moves forward.*)

DEIRDRE: (*As Berengaria.*)

Here I, Berengaria, Richard's Queen, do appear,
King Richard, come close, come here.
Here, my husband, and boldly play thy part,
That all the people present may see thy wonderous art.

MICHAEL: (*As Richard I.*)

Here again, King Richard, from Britain I have sprung,
I'll fight the infidel bold, for my wonders have begun:
I'll slit his throat, he shall not fly;
I'll cut him down, or else I'll die.

MAHMOUD: (*As Saladin.*)

King Richard seeks red Muslim blood,
And dares to voice his threats out loud.
That English dog, if he before me stands,
I'll cut down with my courageous hand.
With my saracen dagger and my curved sword
I'll soon break up this Christian horde.
His task is first to scale and crawl
And fight his way through mighty Acre's wall.

Look there, King Richard's sister, Joan, by his side,
An arrow for her limb, if I had it, would stem the Jesus
  tide.

FRAN: (*As Joan.*) These Muslims have hardly a weapon left,
Of swords and spears, almost totally bereft,
So now they fight with one eye blind,
Stabbing at shadows, while our archers fire
From superior positions into infidel hinds,
And we catapult fire into the Islamic mire.
There isn't much that they can do.

BARRY: (*As Moor.*) Except hide underground,
And shiver and wait,
To uncover our fate,
Holding our breath, cursing the sound
Of fire and rock, that flies into our homes.
Just as I was hit on this, my leg bone,
By matter from a trebuchet, this Christian stone.
(*BARRY (as Moor) holds up a rock and feels his leg.*)
(*As Moor.*) For this they surely must atone.
Is there a Doctor to be found
All ready, near at hand,
To cure a deep and deadly wound
And help this moorish trader stand!
(*CLIVE (as Doctor) crosses to BARRY, holding an empty
syringe.*)
(*As Moor.*) All ready, near at hand,
To cure a deep and deadly wound
And help this moorish trader stand!
What can you cure?

CLIVE: (*As Doctor.*) All sorts of diseases,
Whatever you pleases,
The phthisic, the palsy, and the gout.
Whatever the disorder, I could soon draw it out.

BARRY: (*As Moor.*) What is your fee?

CLIVE: (*As Doctor.*) Alas, no fee can buy your rejuvenation,
There's no medication for this broken nation.
Except that offered up by quacks.
Listen, I'll acquaint you with the facts:
You see, our medicines are all gone,
There's nothing left, you'll have to hang on,

This city is bled dry of cures and remedies,
You'll have to travel overseas.

BARRY: (*As Moor.*) But how? I'm trapped here, While
Christians lay siege and fill us with fear. There's no way I
can get out.

CLIVE: (*As Doctor.*) Of that, I have no doubt.

BARRY: (*As Moor.*) We're all starving in this city,
Disease and hunger everywhere you look,
Two years, trapped, like this, without pity,
Genocide,

CLIVE: (*As Doctor.*) And they'll get off the hook.
Wars of attrition, started, and then,
Fought and re-fought again,

BARRY: (*As Moor.*) And again.

CLIVE: (*As Doctor.*) Chlidren murdered, women and men,
But the world just watches it happen, again,

BARRY: (*As Moor.*) And again.

CLIVE: (*As Doctor.*) Wars of avarice, in the name of some God.

BARRY: (*As Moor.*) Fought and re-fought,

CLIVE: (*As Doctor.*) Don't you find that odd?

BARRY: (*As Moor.*) Outside these walls the elderly butchered,

CLIVE: (*As Doctor.*) Not even burried under sod.

BARRY: (*As Moor.*) While the world just watches the torture,

CLIVE: (*As Doctor.*) Don't you find that odd?

BARRY: (*As Moor.*) What's in a name? What's in a religion?

CLIVE: (*As Doctor.*) You're Muslim, others Jewish, that's their
ammunition.
I'm getting shot at, a humanitarian doctor here.

BARRY: If they aren't stopped soon,

CLIVE: We'll all be dead come the end of the year.

BARRY: (*As Moor.*) But before all this we lived side by side,
Just got on with things, there was nothing to hide.

CLIVE: (*As Doctor.*) That was then, this is now. And I bet
When it's over, the world will soon forget.

BARRY: (*As Moor.*) At the moment it's survival, just to eat and
to drink,
There's no time for commerce, no chance to think.

CLIVE: (*As Doctor.*)
But the cisterns are parched, the provender gone,
No blockade running ships can get through,

BARRY: (*As Moor.*) So we suck the skin from rotten lemons.

CLIVE: (*As Doctor.*) Well, what would you do?

BARRY: (*As Moor.*) We eat the leather from our shoe.

CLIVE: (*As Doctor.*) Well, what would you do?

(*MAHMOUD (as Saladin) crosses to BARRY and CLIVE with a bottle of medicine.*)

MAHMOUD: (*As Saladin.*)

Here come I, Saladin, I can cure your ills, see,

If this war you'll wage with me.

And take up arms with King and peasant,

Your fighting fist is all my fee,

I'll charge you now not even one bezant.

I have a little bottle of Elucumpane:

Here Moor, take a little of this flip-flop,

Pour it down thy tip-top,

Then rise up and fight with me.

BARRY: (*As Moor.*) This thing I'll do,

For what have I to lose,

I'll run this invader through,

It's his death I choose.

(*MAHMOUD (as Saladin) gives BARRY (as Moor) some medicine.*)

MAHMOUD: (*As Saladin.*) I now guarantee,

Your complete recovery. Rise up and fight with me.

MICHAEL: (*As Richard I.*)

Here am I, King Richard, a worthy champion bold,

With my sword and spear I've won many crowns of gold.

And now the port of Acre, I've brought close to slaughter,

And with the scent of victory I steal every Muslim's daughter.

The plan I have is really of the very simplest kind,

My knights take Muslim women and rape and rape and rape,

Until one glorious day the infidel females find

They're pregnant, but there's work to be done, they must not escape.

Keep them under lock and key, till it's too late to abort,

Then send them out to wander about and very soon they'll find,

As unclean women, they and their offspring are not
welcomed by their kind.

Call it, theological terrorism, now there's a thought.

AYESHA: (*As Pregnant Woman.*)

While the male prisoners are starved and tortured,
The Crusader's enter womankind's virgin orchard.
Raped and raped and raped again,
What am I to do?
I'm pregnant now, by Crusading men,
Who do I turn to?
Sent back to the city,
Some seven or eight months gone,
No one will take pity,
On this women's bastard daughter or son.
Raped and raped and raped again,
What am I to do?

BARRY: (*As Moor.*) No good coming here,
We want nothing to do with you.

AYESHA: (*As Pregnant Woman.*) Food, please feed me, some
clothes for my back,
Shelter from the cold, some protection from attack.

CLIVE: (*As Doctor.*) No one will permit it.

AYESHA: (*As Pregnant Woman.*) I cannot wish my womb to
shrivel and dry.

CLIVE: There's nothing I can do. Your unborn child offends
their eye.

AYESHA: (*As Pregnant Woman.*)

I've become an outcast amongst my own people,
A Mother of a new generation of inbuilt outcasts.
Women destroyed by this fundamentalist, sexual cull,
Shunned here, spat on there, made impure by our past.
And the children, the hope of a nation,
Unclean by means of their begetting.
For us there'll be no forgetting,
Of procreation as religious ammunition.

MICHAEL: (*As Richard.*) We've starved the enemy night and
day
And pummelled them with stone,
No one heard their prayers for us to go away,
Not one single siege life-line was thrown.

Now I, King Richard, bestride the Acre wall,
Betimes my men will force into the garrison,
Of bloodletting there'll be no saracen comparison,
We'll show no pity, this city will very soon fall.

MAHMOUD: (*As Saladin.*)

Here come I, Saladin, Muslim warrior,
Now we'll find out who'll be the sorrier,
I'll fight King Richard, who is my foe,
And make him yield before I go:
He brags to such a high degree
He thinks that none can do the like of he.

MICHAEL: (*As Richard I.*)

Where is the infidel that would before me stand?
I'll cut him down with my chivalrous hand.

MAHMOUD: (*As Saladin.*) Not before I avenge the evil you've
done.

MICHAEL: (*As Richard I.*)

What's that? I'm not the only guilty one.
You're just as cruel and ruthless as me.

MAHMOUD: (*As Saladin.*) God's on my side,

MICHAEL: (*As Richard I.*) About that we'll see.

(*MICHAEL, as Richard I, and MAHMOUD, as Saladin, fight.
MAHMOUD, as Saladin, is eventually defeated and falls to one
knee. During the fight the characters begin to remove each others'
twelfth-century costumes, the canopy is lifted to reveal the bus
and the church façade gradually recedes into the rock face so
that by the end of the mummers' play we have returned to the
original setting.*)

MAHMOUD: (*As Saladin.*) Oh! Pardon me, King Richard,
pardon of thee I crave. Oh! Pardon me this night and I
will be thy slave.

MICHAEL: (*As Richard I.*)

I'll never pardon a saracen knight,
So rise thou up and try thy might.

(*They fight again. Once again MICHAEL, as Richard, is
victorious.*)

(*As Richard I.*)

Now you are defeated, but your garrison may go free,
If you restore the True Cross, release all Christian
prisoners, and pay 200,000 bezants to me.

MAHMOUD: (*As Saladin.*)

    I am defeated, to your price I must agree.

    But our battles are not yet over, of that, in time, you'll see.

MICHAEL: (*As Richard I.*) So ladies and gentlemen your sport
    has almost ended,

    Except to now explain, that this Muslim soon offended

    Me, Good King Richard, when he failed to pay even one
    bezant,

    And I took offence against the Islamic crescent.

    So in the year of our Lord, 1191,

    The list of Saracen dead multiplied under Palestine's sun,

    There it was, a lesson plain to see,

    The slaughter of 3,000 infidel prisoners, by me.

    (*By now the characters are back in their ordinary costume, the
    church façade has gone and the bus can once again be seen.*)

MAHMOUD: (*Mumbling to himself.*) All ready, near at hand,

    To cure a deep and deadly wound

    And make the champion stand...

    ...Then rise up and fight again.

FRAN: Do you think he's alright?

CLIVE: I don't know, he's just gibbering.

    (*BARRY looks into MAHMOUD's eyes.*)

BARRY: He's gone. He's on another planet.

DEIRDRE: What are we going to say to the blokes who come
    to tow us?

CLIVE: If they ever get here.

MICHAEL: We'd better get rid of him.

AYESHA: What?

MICHAEL: We could do without awkward questions?

AYESHA: Get rid of him?

MICHAEL: In the cave. They won't look in there.

AYESHA: Don't be ridiculous. We can't just leave him here.

CLIVE: We've got to do something.

AYESHA: I'll take responsibility.

MICHAEL: I'm not letting you take chances with my life. He's
    a bloody liability. If those people think we've harmed one
    of them.

DEIRDRE: No. She's right, he needs help.

    (*DEIRDRE holds out her hip flask.*)

    Here, give him a drink.

AYESHA: He's Muslim you idiot. We'll just have to hope these other people get here soon, he looks on the verge of collapse.

MAHMOUD: I'll be alright.

AYESHA: Are you sure?

MAHMOUD: Yes.

AYESHA: You're shaking.

(*AYESHA puts an arm around MAHMOUD.*)

MICHAEL: Another one for the harem.

AYESHA: I've had enough of you.

MICHAEL: I can assure you the feeling is mutual…

I could kill him for getting us into this mess.

AYESHA: And what would that achieve?

MICHAEL: A small degree of satisfaction.

MAHMOUD: Go on then. Kill me. I'm waiting. Is there a problem?

MICHAEL: The man's a mental defective.

MAHMOUD: Not frightened are you?

MICHAEL: I'm not frightened of anyone or anything.

Especially jumped up little Arabs like you.

MAHMOUD: So kill me. Rid the planet of one more filthy Arab. Kill me!

DEIRDRE: Hey, come on you two.

MAHMOUD: Can't you do it? You want the gun? I can get the gun. Perhaps you'd like to use it.

MICHAEL: Don't think I wouldn't.

(*MAHMOUD crosses to the bus.*)

DEIRDRE: Will you two stop it. (*Trying to make light of the argument.*) If anyone should be shot around here, it's him.

CLIVE: Me! What have I done?

DEIRDRE: Whinge and moan all bloody day… I'm just joking.

CLIVE: Well, as you brought the subject up, I'm not particularly keen on people like you.

DEIRDRE: 'People like me'… Tell me, Clive, darling, what exactly do you mean by 'people like me'!?

CLIVE: Vulgar, loud-mouthed, vindictive, Antipodean Anglophobes.

DEIRDRE: Michael, would you say that's a fair assessment of my personality?

MICHAEL: Spot on.

DEIRDRE: (*To MICHAEL.*) Are you alright? You shouldn't get worked up.

MICHAEL: I'm sick to death of him. I'm sick to death of his sort. Bloody poor Arabs begging and pestering you everywhere you go. Bloody rich Arabs, swanking about, flashing off their wealth in other people's countries.

DEIRDRE: Come off it, Michael, the Brits have been doing that for generations.

MICHAEL: Don't you start.

(*MAHMOUD takes the gun from beneath the driver's seat. He offers it to MICHAEL.*)

MAHMOUD: Here.

AYESHA: This is getting out of hand. Put it away, Mahmoud.

MAHMOUD: (*To MICHAEL.*) Take it.

MICHAEL: Don't be ridiculous.

MAHMOUD: You want to kill me. So, kill me.

BARRY: Give me the gun.

MAHMOUD: (*To MICHAEL.*) Take it.

MICHAEL: I'm not taking your gun. Now, put it away.

MAHMOUD: Have you never killed before? Because I have. I've killed. Would you like me to show you how?

MICHAEL: You don't scare me.

MAHMOUD: A stone hit me, here, between my shoulders. I turned and shot. He was a child. Just a child. Nine, maybe ten years old.

AYESHA: Then was this?

MAHMOUD: Two years ago. When I was in the army, in Gaza.

FRAN: What army?

MAHMOUD: The Israeli army.

DEIRDRE: I thought you were Palestinian?

MAHMOUD: My Father is Palestinian.

FRAN: Then what were you doing in the Israeli army?

MAHMOUD: Serving my country. My Mother is Jewish.

FRAN: Your Father's Palestinian and your Mother's Israeli. So what does that make you?

DEIRDRE: Bloody confused, I should think.

(*DEIRDRE takes a drink from her hip flask.*)

MAHMOUD: Here, please.

DEIRDRE: It's rum.

MAHMOUD: Please.

(*DEIRDRE hands the hip flask to MAHMOUD. He drinks.*)

DEIRDRE: I thought Muslims didn't drink.

MAHMOUD: The Jewish half of me drinks, the Muslim half remains perfectly sober.

AYESHA: I don't see how you can be both Jewish and Muslim.

MAHMOUD: I'm not. I was brought up a jew. My parents families forced my mother and father to part when they found out about them. Hypocrites – my mother's own father was a gentile, a Palestinian Christian, he converted to Judaism so he could marry into the family. They sent my mother to relatives in America, I was born there. We came back here when I was five.

AYESHA: So you're not a practising Muslim?

MAHMOUD: No.

FRAN: What happened to your father?

MAHMOUD: I don't know. I've been searching for him for the past year and a half. I never knew him, only heard stories about him from my mother. She said they were very much in love. Only, she forgot to tell me he wasn't Jewish. She waited until I murdered, until I shot that boy in Gaza City. Then she broke down. He doesn't even know I exist…The boy I killed, he was just copying, just throwing stones. His name was Mahmoud Said. He was a refugee, the child of refugees; just as my mother was the daughter of refugees from Europe. And just as I would have been the son of a refugee if my father had taken me. I've got the blood of almost every religious war ever fought flowing in my veins. The murderer and the victim. Nazi and Jew, Saracen and Crusader, Bosnian and Serb. I live in a land promised to the jews; the scene of Jesus' life; the site of Muhammmad's ascent to heaven. And I am all these people. (*To MICHAEL.*) Here, I give you the gun. Which part of me would you kill? Which part of me would you save?

MICHAEL: I don't want your gun.

MAHMOUD: (*To MICHAEL.*) You think the life of that child was cheap? Compared to you, he's worthless. Yes?

MICHAEL: I never said that.

MAHMOUD: But you're an important man. What was he? Nothing.

MICHAEL: Your words not mine.

MAHMOUD: I think perhaps we should play a game, just to pass the time.

FRAN: Mahmoud, put the gun away.

MAHMOUD: The game is this – If there was someone here now, holding a gun to your head, telling you that you had to select one of your travelling companions to die or everyone here would be killed, who would you choose? (*BARRY makes a grab for the gun but MAHMOUD sees him, turns and points the gun at him.*)
(*To BARRY.*) You first.
(*MAHMOUD picks up the skull and hands it to BARRY.*)
Who would you choose?

BARRY: I wouldn't choose anyone.

(*MAHMOUD fires the gun over BARRY's head.*)

MAHMOUD: Who?

BARRY: You.

MAHMOUD: No, you must choose one of the others. I'm not included.

CLIVE: Just pick someone.

BARRY: (*Pointing to MICHAEL.*) Him.

MAHMOUD: Why?

BARRY: No reason.

MAHMOUD: You must state your reason.

BARRY: He said my poetry was crap.

MAHMOUD: Just that?

MICHAEL: It's because I'm white.

BARRY: It's because you represent Babylon.

MAHMOUD: (*Indicating DEIRDRE.*) What about her?

BARRY: I've only known her half a day.

MAHMOUD: You've only known him half a day, yet you've condemned him. You should consider some of the others. (*Pointing to CLIVE.*) Tell me what you know about him.

BARRY: He's an actor.

MAHMOUD: Would you take him as a friend?

BARRY: No.

MAHMOUD: What don't you like about him?

BARRY: I've had enough of this.

MAHMOUD: Tell me. What don't you like? Something you have observed about this man that explains why you would not seek his company.

BARRY: He's not very intelligent.

CLIVE: What?

MAHMOUD: (*To CLIVE.*) You find that offensive?

CLIVE: I don't care what he thinks.

MAHMOUD: You don't find his remark offensive?

CLIVE: Of course I do.

MAHMOUD: Why?

CLIVE: Because I'm more intelligent than dope-smoking rastafarians like him.

BARRY: What do you know about Haile Selassie? What do you know about rastafarianism?

CLIVE: Enough to understand that it's nothing more than a personality cult.

BARRY: And the worship of Jesus and Mary and Muhammad aren't the same thing?

CLIVE: Of course not.

BARRY: (*To MAHMOUD.*) I changed my mind – he gets it.

MAHMOUD: Give your reason.

BARRY: He's ignorant. People are more complicated than the way they look. Yes, I believe in Jah Ras Tafari; I believe in the word of the Bible; I believe in peace and love. Yes, I am a rastafarian, but I am many more things besides. I believe in many things, I admire many people – poets, athletes, politicians. Derek Walcott, Malcolm X – Malcolm X, an orthodox Muslim. We're all full of contradictions.

MAHMOUD: If that's true isn't he (*Points to CLIVE.*) more than just ignorant? Isn't he (*Points to MICHAEL.*) more than just a symbol of what your culture despises?

MICHAEL: I've already told you why he doesn't like us.

BARRY: To be honest, I don't particularly like any of you.

DEIRDRE: Can we stop this stupid game now?

FRAN: It shouldn't just be a matter of like and dislike. I mean, you have to take into consideration what you perceive to be each person's contribution to life.

DEIRDRE: Don't encourage him.

MAHMOUD: (*To BARRY.*) Well?

BARRY: (*Indicating MICHAEL.*) Him.

MAHMOUD: (*To DEIRDRE.*) You. (*To BARRY.*) Give her the skull.
(*BARRY passes the skull to DEIRDRE.*)

DEIRDRE: I'm having nothing to do with this… Alright then, I'd shoot myself, how's that?

MAHMOUD: No. No suicide.

DEIRDRE: (*Pointing to FRAN.*) Her, then.

FRAN: Why me? I've done nothing to you.

DEIRDRE: You don't have to. I just chose the ugliest person here.

MICHAEL: She's not ugly.

DEIRDRE: No? Well, she looks bloody ugly to me. About as ugly as that tart you call your PA.

MICHAEL: Andrea?

DEIRDRE: Yes, darling, Andrea. (*To MAHMOUD.*) Can I nominate someone who isn't here?

MAHMOUD: No.

DEIRDRE: Shame. Andrea could do with a bullet in the head.

MICHAEL: What's Andrea ever done to you?

DEIRDRE: Sod all. It's what she's done to you that I'm interested in.

MICHAEL: Andrea and I are not, and never have had an affair.

DEIRDRE: That's what you say.

MICHAEL: I don't believe this. You mean you're actually jealous?

DEIRDRE: You've been sleeping with her for at least the last three years, Michael.

MICHAEL: Rubbish.

DEIRDRE: Hobart, 1991. Brisbane, 1992. Paris, 1992. Wellington, 1993… Shall I go on?

MICHAEL: If you know so much, why do you put up with it?

DEIRDRE: Because I enjoy spending your money and fucking your business associates.

MICHAEL: Really? And precisely who have you 'fucked'?
    (*DEIRDRE is silent.*)
    Just as I thought – No one.

DEIRDRE: I don't know what she sees in you.

MICHAEL: Love.

DEIRDRE: Ha. Ha.

MICHAEL: Passion.

DEIRDRE: Passion! Christ, she must be deranged.
    (*MICHAEL snatches the skull from DEIRDRE.*)

MICHAEL: (*Indicating DEIRDRE.*) She's my choice. She's dead.

(*MICHAEL throws the skull back at DEIRDRE.*)

MAHMOUD: Very well. (*To DEIRDRE – indicating MICHAEL.*) And you would choose him to die?

DEIRDRE: I wouldn't give him the pleasure.

MAHMOUD: But you wouldn't be responsible for his death and you could take his wealth.

MICHAEL: She'll be lucky, I've got it all signed over to my son. All she gets when I go is the Modigliani and a kick up the backside.

DEIRDRE: Thank you, Michael. All this from the man who lost every cent of the money my father left to me on the stock market.

AYESHA: I don't know how you put up with a pig like him.

DEIRDRE: Because he's dying.

MICHAEL: I am not dying.

DEIRDRE: He's got cancer of the pancreas.

MICHAEL: The cancer is under control.

DEIRDRE: They removed a tumour, but they can't be certain the cancer's gone. That's why we're here, he wants to be absolved of his sins in the holy city before he meets the great Banker in the sky.

MICHAEL: Rubbish.

DEIRDRE: He wasn't always like this, you know. It's only since he found out about the cancer. That's when he turned pig-ignorant, that's when he started the affair. Believe it or not I actually love the bastard.

MAHMOUD: Who is your choice?

DEIRDRE: I told you (*Indicating FRAN.*) – Her.

FRAN: You are unbelieveable.

DEIRDRE: Listen, I don't like your attitude, right. People like you swan about thinking the world owes you a living, well, it doesn't. You have to participate.

FRAN: I participate…I do… (*She looks around the others for support. She fixes her eyes on AYESHA.*) I do.

AYESHA: You treat religion and philosophy as if they were fashion accessories – One goes out of style, you try another.

FRAN: That simply isn't true.

MAHMOUD: (*To FRAN.*) Your turn.

FRAN: Why are you doing this, Mahmoud?

MAHMOUD: I told you, to pass the time.

FRAN: But, why do you want to upset people?

MAHMOUD: You have the choice of who you kill. I did not.

DEIRDRE: Go on. Get it over with.

FRAN: I would never choose a woman. No matter how wrong their judgement of me might be…Clive.

CLIVE: Why?

FRAN: I don't feel drawn to you. I don't know you. I don't feel I could get to know you. Your death wouldn't hurt me as much as some of the other people here.

CLIVE: Thank you very much.

FRAN: I'm sorry, Clive –

CLIVE: The only reason you're choosing me is because (*Indicating BARRY.*) he's black and all of sudden you feel sorry for *him.* (*Indicates MICHAEL.*)
(*MAHMOUD takes the skull from FRAN and passes it to CLIVE.*)

MAHMOUD: (*To CLIVE.*) What about you?

CLIVE: I couldn't care less. Anyone, except Ayesha.

MAHMOUD: Choose someone.

CLIVE: (*Indicating DEIRDRE.*) Probably her. No. She's an old bag, but she's got a sense of humour. (*To MAHMOUD.*) Can I ask questions?

MAHMOUD: Of course.

CLIVE: (*To DEIRDRE.*) Are you religious?

DEIRDRE: Me? I'm a raving agnostic. Used to sing in a choir when I was a teenager. St Paul's, Church of Australia.

CLIVE: (*To MICHAEL.*) What about you?

MICHAEL: I'm too busy for religion.

CLIVE: (*Indicating DEIRDRE.*) I thought she said –

MICHAEL: I was raised a Catholic, if it came to pistols at dawn I might just request the presence of a Priest.

AYESHA: *Testiculos habet et bene pendentes.*

CLIVE: What?

AYESHA: When they elect a new Pope he has to sit on a special seat with a hole in it so the cardinals can touch him up and proclaim: '*Testiculos habet et bene pendentes.*' A rough translation being: 'Testicles has he and well-hung ones.' It dates from the ninth century when a woman managed to con her way into becoming Pope. It was only when she gave birth in the middle of a papal procession that she was found out.

FRAN: Really... I never knew that.

AYESHA: A minor case of sexual discrimination by Catholic standards.

MICHAEL: Of course, Islam treats men and women as equals. That's why the men marry several women at once. Now, coming from a civilized society, I happen to think that's wrong.

AYESHA: I agree, polygamous marriage is awful – much better to be an adulterer.

CLIVE: (*Pointing to MICHAEL.*) Him. I want him to be killed. When I was about eight, a group of Catholic boys used to taunt me and chase me on my way home from primary school.

MICHAEL: What the hell has that got to do with me?

CLIVE: You're Catholic.

MICHAEL: So bloody what?

CLIVE: They made my life a misery just because the school I went to was C of E.

MICHAEL: Boys bully boys.

CLIVE: This is my chance to get them back.

MICHAEL: But you're not getting them, you're getting me.

CLIVE: Next best thing.

BARRY: That's the kind of stupid reasoning that perpetuates all the hate in the world.

CLIVE: Hold the front page – Black, Islamic, Rastafarian, poet, footballer discovers what's wrong with humanity.

FRAN: I'm Catholic. Why not kill me?

MICHAEL: There. Kill her.

CLIVE: No.

MICHAEL: Why? We're both Catholic. What's the difference?

FRAN: I stayed with a Lutheran family on a German exchange once, the kids in that family were really horrible to me, but I don't hate all Protestants or all Germans because of it.

CLIVE: He asked for my choice and I've given it. I'm sorry if you don't like it.

MICHAEL: But she chose you, she's Catholic, what more do you need? Surely you should choose her.

CLIVE: No.

FRAN: He's right. You should choose me.

CLIVE: Alright then, you want me to choose you, I'll choose
you. I don't bloody care. (*To MAHMOUD – indicating FRAN.*)
Her.

AYESHA: I'll say this for you, Clive, once your mind's made
up, there's no telling what you'll decide.

CLIVE: What's that supposed to mean?

AYESHA: It means you're incapable of making any decisions
for yourself.

CLIVE: Alright then, I'll choose him.

AYESHA: I give up.

CLIVE: Well, what do you want me to say? Because if all you
intend to do is have a go at me I could quite happily do
without you as well.

BARRY: And me?

CLIVE: And you. And him, and her, and her. The whole
bloody lot of you.

MAHMOUD: Well?

CLIVE: (*Indicating MICHAEL.*) Him.

MAHMOUD: (*To AYESHA.*) Your turn.

(*CLIVE passes the skull to AYESHA.*)

AYESHA: I don't want it.

(*AYESHA pushes the skull back at CLIVE. MAHMOUD takes the
skull and places it at AYESHA's feet.*)

MAHMOUD: Speak.

AYESHA: I would have thought it was obvious.

MICHAEL: And I thought you wanted to be one of my wives.
How could our relationship have gone so sour so soon?

MAHMOUD: I make that three people who choose you to die.

MICHAEL: Enemies are sometimes neccessary to succeed in
this world.

(*MAHMOUD holds the gun to MICHAEL's head.*)

MAHMOUD: So you die.

MICHAEL: You wouldn't dare.

MAHMOUD: Wouldn't I?

MICHAEL: In front of all these witnesses.

MAHMOUD: What do I care.

FRAN: Mahmoud, don't do it.

DEIRDRE: Put it down.

MAHMOUD: Why? He chose you to die.

DEIRDRE: It was a game. He didn't mean it.

MAHMOUD: No. No game. (*To MICHAEL.*) Would you like to pray?

MICHAEL: Stop him someone, for Christ's sake!

MAHMOUD: Remember the rules – One person dies or you all die. Any of you tries to stop me and I hunt you all down. (*To MICHAEL.*) Is there anything you want to say? Can you give me a reason why I shouldn't kill you? Perhaps you would like to make a confession?… No confession? No reason to live?

MICHAEL: I know politicians, world leaders, industrialists. Many people rely on me.

MAHMOUD: No. Not good enough.

MICHAEL: My family. I have a son.

MAHMOUD: No.

MICHAEL: If you want money –

MAHMOUD: No bribes.

AYESHA: Mahmoud –

MAHMOUD: My name is Isaac.

(*MICHAEL starts to utter a prayer under his breath.*)

MAHMOUD: Listen… Words to God. Does he hear you?

DEIRDRE: Stop this. We're rich. You can have anything you want. Name your price. Anything.

MAHMOUD: No bribes.

DEIRDRE: It's not him offering it, it's me.

MAHMOUD: No. I don't need your money or your paintings or your houses. I don't kill for money or religion. This is an act of purification. Without faith or greed, because murder in the name of faith soon becomes greed, and greed soon becomes your faith.

(*DEIRDRE goes to move towards MAHMOUD. MAHMOUD pushes the gun into the back of MICHAEL's neck.*)

MAHMOUD: (*To DEIRDRE.*) Stay there.

MICHAEL: Please… No…

MAHMOUD: Don't beg, it doesn't become you.

AYESHA: Don't do it.

MAHMOUD: (*To MICHAEL.*) I'll make you one last offer – You kill me… Did you hear? Take the gun and shoot me. I die in your place.

(*MAHMOUD stands back from MICHAEL and offers him the gun.*)

Take it. Kill me, and you live.

(*MICHAEL slowly takes the gun and turns it on MAHMOUD.*)

There, not so hard is it.

DEIRDRE: Don't shoot, Michael.

MAHMOUD: We have a deal.

DEIRDRE: Michael, there's no need for anyone to get shot.

MAHMOUD: Kill me.

(*MICHAEL is nervous, he stares from person to person, unsure about what to do.*)

DEIRDRE: You've got the gun, just keep it, nothing can happen.

(*MICHAEL slowly begins to lower the gun. MAHMOUD jumps at MICHAEL and MICHAEL fires the gun. MAHMOUD falls. Silence.*)

Oh Christ, what have you done…

MICHAEL: It wasn't my fault. I didn't mean to do it. He made me. He jumped at me. You saw him. I was putting the gun down. I wasn't going to do anything. He made me do it. Oh God…

(*MICHAEL throws down the gun and buries his head in is hands. FRAN kneels beside MAHMOUD.*)

(*To DEIRDRE.*) I could never kill anyone, you know that.

FRAN: He's dead. You shot him.

DEIRDRE: You saw what happened, the bloke jumped at him. It was an accident.

AYESHA: Accident!

CLIVE: I don't believe this.

MICHAEL: It was a reflex. I thought… I was confused, I thought he might try to take the gun off me, I couldn't help it. You saw what he did to me.

AYESHA: He was just using you to make a point.

MICHAEL: He was going to kill me.

AYESHA: Of course he wasn't going to kill you.

MICHAEL: I'm sorry… I'm sorry…

(*AYESHA crosses to MAHMOUD.*)

BARRY: (*To MICHAEL.*) You are damned.

AYESHA: He's still breathing. (*Stands.*) Quick, someone, see if there's anything in the mini-bus, a first aid kit or something to stop the bleeding.

(*MAHMOUD stands.*)

MAHMOUD: Rise up, Lazarus… (*To MICHAEL.*) Here, (*He picks up the gun and tosses it to MICHAEL's feet.*) shoot me again. Perform a miracle, turn blanks into bullets.

(*MICHAEL grabs MAHMOUD and attempts to strangle him.*)

DEIRDRE: No!

AYESHA: Stop him!

(*BARRY, FRAN and CLIVE succeed in pulling MICHAEL off MAHMOUD.*)

MICHAEL: You're evil.

MAHMOUD: Yes, but which part of me is more evil – Muslim, Christian, or Jew?

DEIRDRE: Why don't you shut up!

FRAN: (*To MAHMOUD.*) I thought he'd killed you.

(*MAHMOUD picks up the gun and fires it.*)

MAHMOUD: Blanks – to frighten the wolves. You don't think the people here would waste good bullets on us…

CLIVE: Who the hell do you think you are?

DEIRDRE: That was a cruel trick.

MAHMOUD: Did you really think I was going to kill him? After all I told you. Every day I see the child I murdered, I pray we don't all need such lessons. (*To MICHAEL.*) A game. Just a game.

FRAN: You went too far.

BARRY: No, he was justified.

FRAN: You can't play games like that with people, even when what you're saying is right.

CLIVE: You're lucky we didn't let him strangle you.

MAHMOUD: Perhaps you should've done.

MICHAEL: You won't get away with this. You will not get away with this!

DEIRDRE: Michael… Come on…

(*DEIRDRE leads MICHAEL away from the others.*)

AYESHA: Mahmoud, some of us… I was on your side.

MAHMOUD: Why? Because he was the one I was making an example of instead of you?

CLIVE: There's someone coming.

(*CLIVE points offstage.*)

FRAN: The truck. Come on, let's get cleared up.

CLIVE: Who's going to care about an empty bottle and a bit of orange peel up here.

FRAN: I am.

(*FRAN starts to clear up. AYESHA and BARRY help her. They clear everything away apart from the skull. DEIRDRE puts her things away. MAHMOUD and CLIVE finish changing the tyre. MICHAEL sits apart from the others. Having finished what she is doing FRAN raises her recorder to her lips.*)

DEIRDRE: Don't even think about it!

(*FRAN puts the recorder away. BARRY notices the skull, he stares at it for a moment then bends down and picks it up.*)

BARRY: (*To MICHAEL.*) Here… (*BARRY throws him the skull.*) Something to remind you of the Holy Land.

(*Blackout.*)

THIS OTHER EDEN

Characters

JULIA EDEN
Violinist. English, home counties. Anglican,
Conservative family

KATE DONNELLY
Violinist. Born and brought up in London. Irish,
Catholic family

DAVID BOAM
Cellist. Jewish. Born in England

GORDON CURRAN
Viola player. Scottish Protestant, Trade Unionist family

JAMES*
Organiser of London concert

ANGUS*
Organiser of Glasgow concert

PATRICK*
Radio journalist, Belfast

SECURITY GUARD*
Belfast

GARETH*
A marketing director, Cardiff

* These parts to be played by the same actor and spoken with
an Irish accent.

Note: This play can be performed with or without a string quartet.
If a quartet is used they should play either a selection of existing
compositions or original compositions specifically written for
the production. The pieces should be played between scenes
where indicated.

This Other Eden was first produced at the Lakeside Theatre, University of Essex, on 6th May 1993 with the following cast:

JULIA EDEN,   Elly Crichton-Stuart
KATE DONNELLY,   Fiona Mallin
GORDON CURRAN,   Anthony Roberts
DAVID BOAM,   Robert Orr
JAMES THOROGOOD/ANGUS/PATRICK/
SECURITY GUARD/GARETH,   Cornelius O'Driscoll

Director, Jonathan Lichtenstein
Designer, Clare Birks
Composer, Nick Sifakis

Music performed by The Kingfisher Quartet

ONE

A stage manager positions four chairs centre forestage then exits. JAMES enters onto forestage.

JAMES: We're very privileged to have with us tonight the Eden Quartet... Er... (*He takes a scrap of paper from his pocket and glances at it.*) Over the past few years the Eden Quartet has established a reputation as one of Britain's leading string quartets and their many diverse recordings, from Beethoven to Bartok, Schubert to Schnittke, have met with worldwide acclaim. (*He glances offstage.*) This... This evening's concert is the last in a series that has taken the quartet around Britain performing the work of composers native to England, Scotland, Ireland and Wales. (*He glances offstage.*) Ladies and Gentlemen, Your Royal Highness, the Eden Quartet. (*He applauds.*)

(*JAMES exits. Enter JULIA, DAVID, KATE and GORDON with instruments. JULIA is dishevelled; DAVID has a plaster cast on one of his legs; KATE is wearing an ill-fitting dress very similar to JULIA's; GORDON has a wet patch on the crotch of his trousers. They cross to their seats, acknowledge the audience, then sit. We hear a couple of notes as the musicians check their tuning. There is a brief pause, a reverential silence, then JULIA, as leader of the quartet, ensures she has the musicians' attention before counting them in. The instant before the first note is to be played GORDON stands and starts to walk offstage.*)

JULIA: Gordon!... (*Under her breath.*) Shit! (*Calling out.*) Gordon!

(*GORDON stops, he turns to JULIA.*)

GORDON: I want an apology out of you.

JULIA: Don't be ridiculous, sit down.

GORDON: (*To audience.*) She's been auditioning viola players behind my back –

JULIA: Sit down!

GORDON: (*To audience.*) Didn't tell me a damn thing about it –

JULIA: (*To audience.*) I'm very sorry about this, Ladies and Gentlemen –

GORDON: (*To audience.*) But she couldn't find anyone good enough to replace me... (*To JULIA.*) ...could you, Julia. You bloody need me, and you can't stand to admit it.

JULIA: Why don't you shut up!

GORDON: Why don't *you* shut up!

DAVID: Be quiet.

KATE: Sit down, Gordon.

DAVID: (*To himself.*) This is so embarrassing.

GORDON: I've had it with that neurotic bitch.

JULIA: What did you call me?

GORDON: A bitch. (*To audience.*) She is the most vile, arrogant –

DAVID: That's enough! Gordon, there is an audience out there.

GORDON: So what?

(*DAVID puts his arm around JULIA.*)

JULIA: (*Aggressively.*) Get off! Don't you dare touch me!

KATE: This is ridiculous.

JULIA: (*To GORDON.*) Why do you always have to upset me?

GORDON: Why do you always have to ask me? – I hate your guts, that's why.

DAVID: I've already told you once!

GORDON: Sod off!

DAVID: You're making us look like idiots.

GORDON: That's because you are bloody idiots.

(*DAVID stands menacingly in front of GORDON.*)

DAVID: You've gone too far this time.

GORDON: And what are you going to do about it!?

KATE: Why don't you two grow up.

DAVID / GORDON: (*Together.*) Shut up!

DAVID: (*To KATE.*) If you hadn't told him – You've got a big mouth.

KATE: Oh, piss off, you reptile!

DAVID: You disgust me.

KATE: …You're a sad, sad man, you know that, David?

DAVID: What the hell's that supposed to mean?

KATE: See your therapist about it.

DAVID: You slut!

(*KATE slaps DAVID. DAVID goes to slap her back, but GORDON grabs his hand.*)

Let go!

KATE: I don't need your help.

GORDON: Shut your face!

(*DAVID pulls his hand free and pushes GORDON away.*)

Don't you push me!
(*The following lines between JULIA and KATE / DAVID and
GORDON take place simultaneously and should run into each
other. These two encounters can either escalate into a four cornered
argument or run as written here.*)

DAVID: Pervert!

JULIA: I asked you not to say
anything to him.

GORDON: At least I'm not a
vain bastard like you.

KATE: Tough.

DAVID: I am not vain!

JULIA: God, you can be
ignorant sometimes.

GORDON: Why do you carry
all that hair gel and lipstick
around with you, then?

KATE: It comes naturally in
your prescence.

DAVID: It's not lipstick. I have
cold sores.

JULIA: What do you care
about the auditions? You
don't want to stay in the
quartet.

GORDON: Really?

KATE: It was a matter of
principle.

DAVID: Yes, really. Christ,
you're like a walking fist.

JULIA: And you'd know all
about principles, wouldn't
you!

GORDON: And you're a
wanker.

KATE: What's that supposed to
mean?

DAVID: Yes? Well, you're a
Marxist, Scottish, soccer
hooligan –

JULIA: As if you didn't know.

GORDON: And you're a Jewish, schizophrenic –

KATE: It happened. It's irrelevant. Forget it.

DAVID: Queer –

JULIA: You're jealous, that's all it is.

GORDON: Cardiff, Holywood, Tel Aviv, Falafel –

KATE: Of what?

DAVID: Lunatic –

JULIA: I suppose you're going to tell me it was all David's doing.

(*On hearing his name DAVID's attention turns to KATE and JULIA.*)

DAVID: What?

KATE: You stupid cow!

JULIA: Sticks and stones.

KATE: Piss off back to Surrey.

JULIA: (*Furious.*) Perhaps if you spent as much time practicing the violin as you did being miserable, you might actually be able to play it one day.

KATE: You're not exactly Yehudi Menuhin yourself.

JULIA: At least my playing has individulaity.

KATE: I hate you.

JULIA: (*Through gritted teeth.*) The feeling's mutual.

DAVID: (*To JULIA.*) Calm down.

JULIA: I am calm.

(*DAVID tries to put his arm around JULIA again. She pushes him away.*)

Get off!

KATE: Nice to see you two getting on so well.

DAVID: (*To JULIA.*) We should talk.

JULIA: I'm not interested.

DAVID: Don't be so uptight.

JULIA: Me? Uptight? You're the one who's uptight.

DAVID: Julia…

JULIA: Leave me alone!

DAVID: You're driving me mad. All day you've been acting like this.

JULIA: What do you expect?

DAVID: I think you need something for your nerves.

GORDON: Do us all a favour and take an overdose.

JULIA: That's it. I'm never playing with any of you ever again.

DAVID: Don't be so melodramatic.

JULIA: I mean it!

GORDON: Good.

DAVID: What about the contract?

JULIA: Sod the contract! I've had enough.

(*JULIA runs off. DAVID goes to follow her.*)

GORDON: And don't come back!

(*DAVID stops.*)

DAVID: You arsehole!

GORDON: She's completely mad.

DAVID: You can talk.

GORDON: Shut your face, hop-along.

DAVID: At least I didn't piss myself before I came on tonight.

GORDON: She threw wine at me.

DAVID: You could've changed.

GORDON: There wasn't time.

DAVID: Is that right?

GORDON: Would you've preferred it if I'd come on in my underpants? Eh? Eh?... Alright.

(*GORDON starts to undo his trousers.*)

DAVID: No! Stop! Stop! Jesus...

(*DAVID exits. GORDON stops taking his trousers off.*)

GORDON: (*Calling after DAVID.*) I hearby declare my independence from this quartet.

KATE: Happy now?

GORDON: Ecstatic.

(*KATE exits.*)

(*To audience.*) What are you staring at? We're not bloody goldfish!

(*GORDON exits. A stage manager removes the chairs.*)

QUARTET PIECE

TWO: 1

Two weeks earlier.

A dressing room in a concert hall in Glasgow – a table, chairs, a clothes rail and a full length mirror. On the table is a bottle of white wine, paper cups, a quiche and assorted sandwiches. JULIA, DAVID and KATE enter. KATE is carrying a violin case and a plastic carrier bag. DAVID is weighed down by two violins, a cello and a suitcase. He is wearing a pretentious black cape – he has no cast on his leg.

DAVID: (*To audience.*) Nine and a half hours it took us to get here.
(*DAVID puts down the case and the instruments.*)
JULIA: (*To audience.*) A seventeen mile tailback on the M6.
DAVID: (*To audience.*) Two hours just to get through Birmingham. My back's killing me.
(*JULIA kisses DAVID.*)
KATE: (*To audience.*) Nine and a half hours in a Citroen 2CV listening to these two discuss homeopathy and vegetables. It was hell.
(*JULIA crosses to the table and picks up the bottle of wine.*)
JULIA: Lambrusco, I might have guessed. The Scottish always get the wine wrong. (*To audience.*) Chardonnay, I said. (*To DAVID and KATE.*) Even an idiot can tell the difference between Lambrusco and Chardonnay. It's like drinking Lucozade. Honestly… (*She looks in one the sandwiches.*)… (*She looks inside another.*) Chicken… (*She sniffs a third.*) Fish paste… Where's that prat who let us in…
(*JULIA exits.*)
DAVID: Gordon's not here then.
KATE: Not unless he's hiding somewhere.
DAVID: What?
KATE: Nothing.
DAVID: Are you alright?
KATE: I'm fine.
DAVID: Only…in the car. You were a bit quiet.
KATE: I'm fine. (*To audience.*) I'm fine.
DAVID: Is it something I said? Something Julia said?

KATE: David, there's nothing wrong. I'm – just – It was a long drive.

DAVID: Sure. (*He takes out a carob bar.*) Want some carob?

KATE: No thank you. And please take that ridiculous cape off, you look like Count Dracula.

(*DAVID looks hurt.*)

I shouldn't have said that. Sorry.

DAVID: Forget it.

(*DAVID takes off his cape.*)

KATE: David –

DAVID: Forget it.

(*DAVID begins to unpack the suitcase, carefully hanging the clothes on the clothes rail. JULIA re-enters, she strides across the room to the table followed by ANGUS. JULIA holds up the bottle of wine. ANGUS looks at the bottle and then back at JULIA.*)

ANGUS: What?

JULIA: Read the label.

ANGUS: What?

JULIA: Is a one-word vocabulary all you possess?

ANGUS: Lambrusco.

JULIA: Very… We asked for Chardonnay.

ANGUS: The contract said white wine.

JULIA: It said Chardonnay.

ANGUS: The other bands like it.

JULIA: 'The other bands…' We're not a pop group. We're one of Britain's premier string quartets, we have performed all over the world, we have an exclusive recording contract with EMI. Christ knows what we're doing here, but we are here and if we are to remain here I suggest we get one thing straight – We do not drink Lambrusco. (*JULIA gives ANGUS the bottle.*) Change it. And no cheap rubbish.

(*ANGUS turns to go.*)

I haven't finished yet.

(*ANGUS stops.*)

These sandwiches…

(*DAVID joins them and examines the sandwiches.*)

We're vegetarians.

DAVID: Neither fish, nor flesh, nor fowl.

ANGUS: There's cheese.

JULIA: Two, processed cheese, Mother's Pride –

ANGUS: Alright, alright.

(DAVID hands ANGUS the plate of sandwiches. JULIA puts the paper cups on top of the sandwiches.)

JULIA: And get some proper glasses.

(ANGUS exits.)

Where's Gordon?

DAVID: No idea.

JULIA: If he's late… I knew we should never have let him come up here on his own.

(JULIA watches KATE disdainfully as KATE takes a dress out of her carrier bag and hangs it up.)

Perhaps you ought to go and have a look for him.

DAVID: Where?

JULIA: I don't know. In the bar. He's been here all weekend. You know what he's like with his Scottish relatives. If he's drunk… I want these concerts to be a success.

DAVID: We all do… He'll be here soon.

JULIA: David, please…

DAVID: I'm going, I'm going.

(JULIA kisses DAVID. He puts on his cape and exits. JULIA picks up a glossy programme and opens it. She immediately closes it again. Then re-opens it slowly. KATE watches her.)

KATE: What is it?

JULIA: A group of half-naked men prostrating themselves before a doric column.

KATE: *(Peering over JULIA's shoulder.)* Who are they? The Chippendales?

(JULIA looks at the cover.)

JULIA: *(Reading out the name.)* The Wedgewoods.

(KATE laughs.)

It's good to hear you laugh again. You've been very sullen the last couple of days.

(KATE moves away.)

What is it? What's wrong… You can talk to me, you know. We always used to talk.

KATE: When?

JULIA: When we first started playing together.

KATE: We never talked.

JULIA: We used to be very close… Has it got something to do with your sister?

KATE: No.

JULIA: Shall I tell you what I think your problem is?

KATE: Feel free.

JULIA: You need a steady relationship.

KATE: Who with? One of the Wedgewoods?

JULIA: Perhaps there's already someone?

KATE: It's got nothing to do with men.

JULIA: Is it about tomorrow?

KATE: Julia, I could do without this.

> (*GORDON enters. He is carrying a viola case.*)

JULIA: Where have you been?

GORDON: You take the high road and I'll take the low road, And I'll be in Scotland afore ye – About two days afore ye to be precise.

JULIA: You're drunk.

GORDON: No I'm not.

JULIA: I can smell it on your breath.

GORDON: Julia, I haven't had a drink for at least twenty-four hours, so either you've got an incredible sense of smell or I've got very bad breath. (*Holding out an arm.*) Here, do a blood test if you don't believe me. (*To audience.*) She gets so wound up about things.

JULIA: (*To audience.*) I have a problem with stress.
(*To GORDON.*) Do you know how long it took us to get here?

GORDON: No…

JULIA: Nine and a half hours.

GORDON: I suppose that's my fault… You know, there is a bit of a funny smell in here. Sort of sickly-sweet.

JULIA: It's Juniper Berry oil – Gives your spirits a lift; clears your head.

GORDON: Oh no, do me a favour.

JULIA: It's called aromatherapy, Gordon.

GORDON: I know what it's called.

JULIA: Don't sneer then. There's nothing wrong with alternative medicine.

GORDON: Alternative medicine, my arse. Alternative hypochondria more like.

JULIA: Just because I don't fill my body with poisons.

GORDON: Do you want to buy some pheromones?

(*DAVID re-enters.*)

Bloody hell, it's Batman.

DAVID: Very funny. I've been looking for you.

GORDON: Well, I'm bloody glad you didn't find me, dressed like that… Joke, David. Oh, sorry, I forgot, you haven't got a sense of humour.

DAVID: I've got a sense of humour. Thankfully it isn't yours.

GORDON: Shalom, David. Where's the Chardonnay?

JULIA: Someone's gone to get it. They tried to give us Lambrusco.

GORDON: Lambrusco… I like Lambrusco.

JULIA: You would.

GORDON: What's that supposed to mean?

(*DAVID takes his cape off and positions some hair gel and moisturiser on the table.*)

What's that?

DAVID: Hair gel.

GORDON: What's that?

DAVID: E45. Moisturiser.

GORDON: Is this some kind of Jewish ritual?

(*JULIA sits in one of the chairs and kicks off her shoes.*)

JULIA: David…

(*DAVID crosses to JULIA and begins to massage her feet.*)

KATE: (*To audience.*) Reflexology.

GORDON: (*To KATE.*) Good acoustic in there.

KATE: Have you played here before?

GORDON: Years ago, when I was a kid. (*To audience.*) This was the first place I ever played as part of an orchestra, about ten years ago. Tchaikovsky, 1812. We had polystyrene cannons – looked like a stage set for AC/DC. (*To JULIA.*) By the way, we're not doing the Tippett tonight.

JULIA: Don't be ridiculous, of course we're doing it.

GORDON: We can't.

JULIA: What do you mean, 'can't'?

GORDON: They've already put a note in the programme.

JULIA: What?

GORDON: I told them we weren't doing the Tippett.

JULIA: When?

GORDON: Yesterday.

JULIA: Gordon, what are you talking about?

GORDON: I told them we'd be doing a piece by Mackenzie instead.

JULIA: Mackenzie… (*To DAVID.*) Get off. (*Puts her shoes back on.*) Are you mad? We haven't rehearsed that in months.

GORDON: I don't want to do the Tippett. I hate Tippett.

JULIA: So you just decided to change it, without a word to any of us. No, Gordon. You can't do that. Christ…

DAVID: Why didn't you say something if you didn't want to do it?

JULIA: You're beginning to worry me, Gordon. This is totally irrational.

GORDON: We were doing two English pieces – by Tippett and Britten; one Welsh – David Wynne; Maconchy – Irish; and one Scottish – McEwan. This is Scotland. So I figured it was only right to do two Scottish composers instead of two English.

JULIA: We're playing the Tippett. Is that clear? Gordon, are you listening to me?

GORDON: I won't do it.

DAVID: Why?

GORDON: Because it's English.

JULIA: And what do we say when we get back to England? – Sorry, we're sick of Tippett, we only do Scottish composers now!

GORDON: Something like that.

JULIA: You're just trying to upset me aren't you?

GORDON: No.

JULIA: You think by doing this you'll ruin my performance. Not a chance – The more you piss me off the better I'll play.

(*ANGUS enters.*)

ANGUS: Is Côtes du Rhône alright?

JULIA: NO!

(*ANGUS turns to go.*)

Wait. Have you put a note in the programme to say that we're doing Mackenzie instead of Tippett?

ANGUS: What?

JULIA: Take them out again.

ANGUS: Take what out?

JULIA: The notes.

ANGUS: What notes? I don't know what you're talking about. (*JULIA stares at GORDON, a look of realization spreading over her face. She sighs. GORDON grins broadly.*)

GORDON: Got you.

JULIA: You bastard.

ANGUS: Now what have I done?

JULIA: Not you. Get out – Come back. (*Holding up the 'Wedgewoods' programme.*) What's this?

ANGUS: They were here last night.

JULIA: Whatever happened to Art?

ANGUS: It was sold out.

JULIA: I rest my case.

GORDON: What is it?

ANGUS: The Wedgewoods. They're like the Chippendales, except from Dundee.

JULIA: Go away.

(*ANGUS exits. GORDON snatches the 'Wedgewoods' programme from JULIA and looks at it.*)

DAVID: So there isn't a note?

(*JULIA snatches the programme back from GORDON.*)

GORDON: He's quick, isn't he. Tell you something, though, it did cross my mind – changing our programme.

JULIA: I loathe you.

KATE: (*To audience.*) Gordon once smeared my bow with half a jar of vaseline five minutes before a concert.

DAVID: (*To audience.*) One time he got us to do a concert in Sicily. It was only when we got there and these men in suits and dark glasses started to follow us around that we discovered it was a concert organized by the Italian Communist party as a demonstration against the Mafia. I was terrified.

GORDON: (*To audience.*) No social conscience these people.

JULIA: (*To audience.*) Last year he pawned my Stradivarius. He took me to the shop and showed it to me in the window. He'd actually gone to the trouble of paying the pawn broker fifty pounds just to see the look on my face.

KATE: (*To audience.*) Sometimes he goes too far.

DAVID: (*To audience.*) Problem is, for an arsehole, he's one hell of a viola player.

(*Lighting state changes. As GORDON tells the following story the other actors perform it. Music can also be used – either as background or as part of the scenario: for example, tuning up / playing scales during the section about the orchestra.*)

GORDON: I got my first viola when I was six years old from a junk shop in Perth – That's Scotland, not Australia.

(*DAVID, as shopkeeper, hands GORDON his viola.*)

For years I thought I was playing the violin, until one day I managed to summon up the courage to audition for the Perth youth orchestra. You have to understand that no one in my family knew anything about music, except one of my aunts who used to live across the road from Lulu. It wasn't on to admit to kids at school that you were into classical music, it was like signing your own death warrant. Especially the school I went to. It was heavy rock or die. Anyway, this smart arse in the Perth youth orchestra came over…

(*JULIA, as member of the Perth Youth Orchestra, crosses to GORDON.*)

JULIA: (*As Youth.*) How long have you been playing the viola?

GORDON: It's a violin.

JULIA: (*As Youth.*) No it isn't.

GORDON: Yes it is… (*To audience.*) And so it went on. We had this huge argument about it. In the end she called over the guy who ran the orchestra.

(*DAVID, as Youth Orchestra Leader, crosses to GORDON with a violin.*)

DAVID: (*As orchestra leader.*) This is a violin. That is a viola. Why don't you come back when you can tell the difference.

(*DAVID and JULIA move away.*)

GORDON: I never felt so stupid in my whole life. It was two years before I dared go back. I hated the kids in that orchestra, they all came from 'respectable' families and lived in 'nice' houses. My family were lunatic, unemployed, Glasgow Rangers supporters who spent all their benefit money on beer and travelling to Ihrox every other weekend to watch the match. They weren't religious, never went to church or anything. I mean, as far as my dad was concerned being Protestant meant hating anything in green and white hoops. I suppose my family are quite political, in an English-hating, Catholic-hating, Tory-hating, Socialist kind of way. My Uncle Alex was the best. He was a fanatical trade unionist. I suppose I got my politics from him.

(*DAVID as Uncle Alex, crosses to GORDON.*)

DAVID: (*As Uncle Alex. Very animated.*) Contingents from all parts of the Scottish industrial areas set out for Glasgow, 3,000 marchers. However, when the marchers reached Perth, there were difficulties placed in their way in respect of accommodation. But the mass support of the Perth workers was soon mobilised and by the end of the day the corporation authorities were forced to give them somewhere to stay…

(*DAVID moves away.*)

GORDON: I used to think all that stuff was great. Still do… Who else? My sister – My sister was a mad bitch when she was a kid.

(*KATE, as GORDON's sister, steps forward.*)

She spent half her time stealing ciggies from eight year olds and the rest screaming abuse at Catholics.

KATE: (*As GORDON's sister.*) Shove your transubstantiation up your arse!

GORDON: I don't think she actually knew what transubstantiation meant, it was enough that it was something Catholic. All things Catholic had to be shoved up your arse as far as she was concerned.

KATE: (*As GORDON's sister.*) Papist bastard!

JULIA: (*As Adversary.*) Calvinist slag!

KATE: (*As GORDON's sister.*) Shove it up your arse!

GORDON: I broke my collar bone because of her – when some left-footer she'd been having a go at shoved me off my bike. She works in local government now – community liason officer.

(*KATE moves away. DAVID, as GORDON's brother, steps forward.*)

I had a brother too. I say 'had' because he died in a motorcycle accident when he was nineteen. He gave me a real hard time about music.

DAVID: (*As GORDON's brother.*) Why don't you listen to some proper bands – Led Zepplin, Whitesnake, Wild Hog...

GORDON: Wild Hog were his band. He played the guitar, badly. (*To brother.*) I prefer Shostakovitch.

DAVID: (*As GORDON's brother.*) Are you a poof or something?
(*DAVID moves away.*)

GORDON: I'm bisexual – Not that your sexual orientation has anything to do with the appreciation of classical music, you understand... Let me tell you about Douglas. Douglas used to hang around the public lavatories in Perth.
(*DAVID, as Douglas, loiters behind GORDON.*)
If someone he liked went in for a slash he used to follow them; he'd stand at a respectable distance and make out he was taking a piss.
(*DAVID, as Douglas, mimes standing at a urinal.*)
That's how I first met him, he was stood about three urinals down from me, watching me, obviously not taking a piss himself, just staring over his shoulder at me. Nothing happened, but when I went back the next day he was there again.
(*GORDON stares at him.*)

DAVID: (*As Douglas.*) What are you staring at?

GORDON: You.

DAVID: (*As Douglas.*) Well... Are you just going to stare or are you going to do something about it?

GORDON: I decided I'd do something about it... So I went into one of the cubicles with him.
(*DAVID, as Douglas, caresses GORDON.*)
It was great.
(*DAVID moves away from GORDON.*)
Anyway, when I went home my girlfriend, Sandra, was waiting for me outside the house.

KATE: (*As Sandra.*) Where have you been?

GORDON: None of your business.

KATE: (*As Sandra.*) I've been waiting out here half an hour.

GORDON: Sandra Nunn – She wasn't Catholic, although she might just as well have been for all the abuse she got about her name.

KATE: (*As Sandra.*) Are you going to keep me standing out here all night?

GORDON: We went in the house. No one was home so I gave her a glass of my mother's Drambuie. But just as we were about to get down to it on the kitchen floor Mother got home early from her bingo.

JULIA: (*As Mother.*) Gordon!

GORDON: She gave me one hell of a talking to.

JULIA: (*As Mother.*) You filthy minded degenerate wee bastard. You've got a one track bloody mind, that's your problem. I've a good mind to take you over my knee, big as you are. Just you wait till your father gets back from his darts, he'll kick you all the way to Inverness…

GORDON: If she's like this when she catches me with Sandra, I thought to myself, what would she do if she caught me and Douglas… She threw us out.

JULIA: (*As Mother.*) Get out, both of you!

(*JULIA, as Mother, pushes GORDON and KATE, then moves away. Fairground music / 'Saturday Night Fever' in background.*)

GORDON: That was the same night I discovered I hadn't been blessed with a cast-iron constitution. After eight pints of heavy and sweet and sour chicken balls from the Wah Hong take-away, me and Sandra went to the fair. It was quite late when we got there and the fair was closing down for the night, but the bloke on the thing with all the swings hanging from chains that goes round in circles, you know the thing, he says he's going to do one more ride, special double length for the price of one go. So me and Sandra get on.

(*GORDON and KATE, as Sandra, mime getting on the cyclo-swing.*)

There's hardly anyone else about, just a few kids and another couple sat right behind us.

(*JULIA and DAVID, as the other couple, get on the cyclo-swing behind GORDON and KATE.*)

It was alright to start with, I didn't even mind that they were playing 'Saturday Night Fever' on the decrepit public address system. Anyway, about the tenth time round, the swings are flying way out, and I start to feel a bit queasy. Sandra's having a great time, the couple behind us are laughing and shouting, but I'm going green. I think to myself it's got to stop soon, it can't go on much longer…

But it just keeps going round and round and round and round. That's when I remember what the man said, about a special double length ride. And I start to hughie. But, you know, it's interesting how your reflexes work, self preservation and all that, because, you see, I didn't want to get covered in sick so every time I hughied I caught it in my hands and threw the hughie over my shoulder. Hughie! (*He mimes being sick into his hands.*) Woof! (*He mimes throwing the sick over his shoulder.*) Hughie! (*He mimes being sick into his hands.*) Woof! (*He mimes throwing the sick over his shoulder.*) Hughie! (*He mimes being sick into his hands.*) Woof! (*He mimes throwing the sick over his shoulder.*) You should've heard the couple behind us screaming. Hughie flying at them and there's nothing they can do to get out the way... Me and Sandra split up soon after that.

(*Lights down.*)

QUARTET PIECE

TWO : 2

As before. After the Glasgow concert. They are putting their instruments away. DAVID puts his arm around JULIA.

DAVID: Brilliant.

(*GORDON copies DAVID by putting his arm around KATE.*)

GORDON: Brilliant.

JULIA: Don't spoil it, Gordon... (*To DAVID.*) Why can't we always play as well as that?

KATE: It was the best we've played in a long time.

GORDON: We should relocate in Scotland.

DAVID: The audience were very appreciative.

JULIA: Let's not get into all that again.

GORDON: What's wrong with Scotland?

DAVID: Nothing – If you like wearing skirts and eating sheep's stomach.

GORDON: You're just jealous... Celtiphobic.

DAVID: What?

JULIA: Anyway, there's a very good reason for not relocating.

GORDON: Is that right?

JULIA: Yes. It hasn't been confirmed yet, but... (*To DAVID.*)
Should I tell them?

DAVID: I don't see why not. They've got to know sooner or
later.

KATE: Tell us what?

GORDON: Please don't tell us you're going get married, I don't
think my stomach could take it.

JULIA: No. It's not that. Although, David and I have
provisionally agreed to discuss the possibility of perhaps
getting engaged at some point over the next couple of
years.

GORDON: You two are so impetuous.

KATE: So, what's this thing you've got to tell us?

JULIA: It's not finalized, but it looks like we've secured a
sponsorship deal.

KATE: Sponsorship?

GORDON: Why weren't we told about this?

KATE: What sort of sponsorship deal?

JULIA: With a soft drinks company.

GORDON: You know what I think about sponsorship.

DAVID: You'll feel differently when you've got an extra couple
of grand in your pocket.

GORDON: It's prostitution. I won't be a part of this. The state
should support the arts, we're not an advertising agency.

JULIA: I knew he'd be difficult.

DAVID: When are you going to realise things have changed?

GORDON: I haven't changed. I'm not a *laissez-faire* musician.
When I play music it's for people who want to listen,
not for some fat bastard executive sat on his arse in a
boardroom somewhere.

DAVID: Gordon –

GORDON: I'm not going round with Coca Cola tattooed on
my forehead, thank you.

DAVID: Gordon, your kind of politics are dead and buried.

GORDON: My kind of politics... My kind – What are you
talking about?

DAVID: You know perfectly well what I'm talking about.
Socialism.

GORDON: You bourgeois bastards are all the same.

DAVID: What's all this 'bourgeois' crap? You're just as 'bourgeois' as I am.

GORDON: How the hell do you work that out?

DAVID: What's classical music if not elitist and bourgeois?

GORDON: I'm bringing classical music to the masses.

DAVID: You and Nigel Kennedy, eh?

GORDON: Piss off.

DAVID: You're just as middle class as he is.

GORDON: No I'm not!

DAVID: You are! You both put on stupid accents –

JULIA: Gordon, we're just trying to get some money behind us, that's all. Balls Brothers are a very reputable drinks company.

GORDON: Balls! Did you say Balls?

JULIA: They have an Impressionist painting on the back of every bottle.

GORDON: I wouldn't care if they had a picture of Maggie Thatcher's tits!

JULIA: Philistine.

GORDON: What have you got against the Philistines? What have they ever done to you?

JULIA: Don't be so pedantic.

GORDON: If I could be granted just one wish before I die, it'd be for Scotland to be set adrift so we could get away from thick, English Tory bastards like you.

JULIA: There's no need to be like that.

GORDON: (*To audience.*) I hate the English. In 1975 when England beat Scotland 5–1 at Wembley, me and my sister locked ourselves in the garden shed and wouldn't come out for two days. We near froze to death.

JULIA: (*To DAVID.*) Let's get out of this place.

DAVID: (*To GORDON.*) Are you going to apologize to Julia?

GORDON: Sorry for not being English, Julia.

JULIA: Thank God for small mercies.

DAVID: Get your things Kate, we're going.

KATE: Don't talk to me like that, you sound like my father. (*Lighting state alters. During the following section Scottish dance music can be heard in the distance.*)

GORDON: When I was ten my father got a job in a cement factory and we had to move to Coventry. It was terrifying.

For the first few weeks I didn't dare open my mouth for fear of my accent being heard. I felt angry. I didn't want to be there. Most of the kids were alright, but some of them…

DAVID: (*As English kid.*) Piss off back to Scotland, Jock strap!

KATE: (*As English kid.*) Kick him in the bagpipes!

GORDON: The more they had a go at me, the more Scottish I became. My accent got heavier; my clothes turned tartan; my sister gave me a tragic Rod Stewart haircut. I felt pushed into a corner, I had to come out fighting. So I did, literally. Scrap after scrap after scrap.

DAVID: (*As English kid.*) Hey, Jock!

GORDON: Wham!

KATE: (*As English kid.*) Where's your kilt?

GORDON: Bam!

JULIA: (*As English kid.*) Excuse me, can you tell me the time, please?

GORDON: Slam! Anything, no matter how innocuous. I hated everyone. It got so a kid only had to look at me and I'd have a go at him. I became the hard man. A tartan scarf round my wrist and the names of the entire 1978 Scotland World Cup squad on every one of my exercise books – just so whenever an English kid looked over my shoulder he'd be reminded they hadn't qualified… My prayers were finally answered after six months when my father had his first heart attack and we came back to Scotland. Not soon enough though.

(*Lighting state returns to normal. Enter ANGUS with Chardonnay, glasses, sandwiches and quiche. JULIA, DAVID and KATE prepare to leave. They all ignore ANGUS.*)

ANGUS: That was a really good concert… I got the chardonnay… Assorted vegetarian sandwiches… Proper glasses…

(*They all ignore him.*)

JULIA: (*To DAVID.*) Where are we staying?

DAVID: Some place outside Stranraer, about fifty or sixty miles from here.

ANGUS: Don't you want it?

(*They still ignore him.*)

JULIA: (*To DAVID, quietly.*) Is Gordon coming with us?

DAVID: No idea.

JULIA: Ask… Ask him.

GORDON: No, I'm not.

DAVID: How are you going to get there?

GORDON: Roller skates. Don't panic, I'll be there.

ANGUS: Do you want to take it with you?

KATE: What time's the ferry in the morning?

DAVID: (*Staring at GORDON.*) Early.

GORDON: What you looking at me for?

DAVID: Because if you don't make it –

GORDON: I'll be there – providing I don't have to do a product endorsement on the way.

DAVID: (*To JULIA.*) Come on.

　　　(*DAVID and JULIA exit.*)

ANGUS: You'll not be wanting this then.

　　　(*KATE and GORDON ignore him. ANGUS exits.*)

KATE: Why do you have to be so aggressive?

GORDON: They get on my nerves sometimes. Telling us what to do and how to do it, like we haven't got a clue. They just use us.

KATE: They're ambitious.

GORDON: And that gives them the right to treat us like shit? I don't like this sponsorship business.

KATE: Don't pretend you couldn't do with the money.

GORDON: That's got nothing to do with it.

KATE: Gordon… Oh, what's the point.

GORDON: What's your problem anyway? You've been as miserable as sin all night.

KATE: It's nothing to do with you…

GORDON: It's Belfast, isn't it? You don't want to go.

KATE: I'll see you tomorrow.

　　　(*Re-enter JULIA.*)

GORDON: Now what?

JULIA: The car won't start.

　　　(*Lights down.*)

QUARTET PIECE

THREE : 1

A dressing room in a concert hall in Belfast. KATE stands apart from DAVID and JULIA. Altered lighting state. The violin is playing one of the pieces from Elgar's 'Enigma Variations'.

KATE: One of my first memories is of my parents having a blazing row.

(*DAVID, as KATE's Dad, and JULIA, as KATE's Mum, move forward.*)

I can even put a date to it: Monday January thirty-first, 1972. I found out later this was the day after British troops shot dead thirteen people in Derry – Bloody Sunday. On that same Sunday night Dad conducted Elgar's 'Enigma Variations' at the Royal Albert Hall, I think that was what they were arguing about.

DAVID: (*As Father.*) What was I supposed to do?

JULIA: (*As Mother.*) You could've made a statement or something.

DAVID: (*As Father.*) What good would that have done?

JULIA: (*As Mother.*) I don't understand how you could just ignore it.

DAVID: (*As Father.*) I didn't know what was happening.

JULIA: (*As Mother.*) Liar.

DAVID: (*As Father.*) It's the truth. I was there from ten in the morning till midnight. I didn't hear the news all day.

JULIA: (*As Mother.*) You turned a deaf ear to it.

DAVID: (*As Father. To audience.*) Half the orchestra had flu. I spent all day on the telephone, ringing every musician within a fifty mile radius of London trying to find replacements.

JULIA: (*As Mother.*) How can you talk about it like that, like it's just another musical anecdote?

DAVID: (*As Father.*) I didn't know.

JULIA: (*As Mother.*) I don't believe you.

(*DAVID and JULIA move away. The violin fades.*)

KATE: My Father had an international reputation as a conductor. I hardly ever saw him when I was growing up.

Mum was, still is, a music teacher at St Mary's Roman Catholic Primary School in Hammersmith. She's what you might call a fundamentalist. Every wall in our house had a virgin, a crucifix, or a Pope on it. Bible readings at bedtime instead of Paddington Bear. Benedictions instead of Brownies. I knew it was wrong to have an abortion before I even knew the facts of life… Mum had been an opera singer, the only time there was any light in her eyes was when she used to talk to us about the opera… Dad was much older than her – eighteen, nineteen years. He was from Dublin. Mum's family were originally from County Down. Dad came to England in the early sixties to teach at college, met Mum and never went back… We lived in Shepherds Bush, in London. 'We' – Dad, when he was there, my mum, my older sister Anna, and yours truly. Me and Anna, somewhat influenced by our father – that's Dad, not the Supreme Being – we both wanted to play the violin. She's a soloist now. Very successful…

(*Fade up sound of transistor radio playing 'Starman' by David Bowie.*)

Dad used to make us practise the violin for an hour after school every day. Sometimes I couldn't be bothered to start straight away and I'd listen to the radio for a while.

(*DAVID, as KATE's Dad, moves forward. He looks up to an imagined window from where the music is playing, a scowl on his face.*)

But Anna always got straight down to her scales.

(*JULIA, as Anna, moves forward. The sound of a young girl practising scales on her violin mixes with the DAVID Bowie song.*)

DAVID: (*As Father.*) Turn that noise off. Off do you hear…

(*The radio is turned off. The violin continues to play in the background, gradually shifting from scales into a piece of Irish music.*)

(*As Father.*) Your sister's trying to practise. (*To audience.*) Listen to her, isn't she exquisite. She has a special gift for music. The ability to be different. Unique. There are great things ahead for Anna, believe me, great things.

KATE: He used to say things like that in front of me all the time. Never about me, even when I practised all day.

I tried so hard to please him. It broke my heart... He must've known it would upset me. He always praised Anna, encouraged her, helped her. She was the gifted one, the prodigy. She was the one my Father sent to the academy for special lessons, not me.

DAVID: (*As Father. To JULIA, as Anna.*) I've had a word with Collins at the academy. He was very impressed with your playing, Anna. He'll be taking you as a private student from next term.

JULIA: (*As Anna.*) Brilliant.

(*JULIA, as Anna, throws her arms around DAVID, as Father, and kisses him. She turns and looks at KATE.*)

(*As Anna.*) What about Kate? Is she going to audition as well?

DAVID: (*As Father.*) She'll be staying with Rosemary Stevens.

JULIA: (*As Anna.*) She hates it there.

DAVID: (*As Father.*) Kate lacks commitment. There's nothing wrong with Rosemary. Kate doesn't have the same application as you, that's all.

KATE: So I had to make do with Rosemary Stevens and her revolting cats – Dvorak, Smetana, Amadeus – whoever heard of a cat called Amadeus? I hated cats, but he still made me go. Anna and I started to fall out a lot after she started at the academy. She would never share with me the things she learned there.

JULIA: (*As Anna.*) What's it got to do with you?

KATE: I couldn't keep up with her. When I went to other kid's birthday parties, she practised. When I went to buy clothes, she practised. When I watched TV, she practised. (*JULIA moves away.*)

Dad just didn't seem to care. I wouldn't do a thing I was told at home; I played truant from school; smoked Number Six by the van-load; I even ran away – twice. I made everyone's life a misery... I've never been to Ireland before. I've always felt too embarrassed, embarrassed by him and all the praise that the Irish heap on his shoulders. I'm embarrassed to be in my own country. Isn't that pathetic...

(*DAVID moves away. Lighting state returns to normal. GORDON enters. JULIA is eating from a Tupperware container.*)

GORDON: Haven't they brought any food yet?

(*GORDON watches JULIA as she eats.*)

I'm starving.

(*JULIA passes GORDON the container.*)

JULIA: Here.

(*GORDON looks at the food.*)

GORDON: What is it?

JULIA: It's vegetarian couscous.

GORDON: Looks like budgie food to me.

JULIA: It's a damn sight healthier than all the meat you throw down your throat.

(*GORDON eats some couscous.*)

DAVID: Hey, listen to this…

GORDON: It tastes like budgie food.

DAVID: (*Reading from the magazine.*) Pisces. You probably have something to celebrate with a special person in your life.

(*To JULIA.*) So what is it we've got to celebrate?

(*JULIA kisses DAVID.*)

JULIA: As if you didn't know.

GORDON: I think I'm going to be violently ill.

(*JULIA ignores GORDON's comment.*)

JULIA: What else does it say?

DAVID: (*Reading from the magazine.*) It seems you have recently started a new phase in your life and everything will begin to get better and better. Look out for an unexpected visitor and a big surprise. (*To KATE.*) What are you Kate?

KATE: What?

DAVID: What star sign?

KATE: Scorpio. Don't read it out, please. I'm not interested.

JULIA: Don't be such a bore, Kate.

GORDON: It's all crap anyway.

JULIA: It's harmless enough. It's not as if it's based on a proper birth chart.

GORDON: You mean like Saturn's rising up Uranus.

JULIA: I think there's something seriously wrong with you.

GORDON: I can't help it. It's my star sign… I'm going to find some proper food.

(*GORDON hands the container back to JULIA.*)

GORDON: Want anything?

JULIA: No.

GORDON: (*To DAVID.*) What about Russell Grant?

(*Enter PATRICK. He is carrying a microphone and cassette recorder.*)

PATRICK: Patrick Kearns, BBC Radio Belfast, I was wondering if I could have a quick interview.

GORDON: I'm all yours.

DAVID: I thought you were going out.

GORDON: No rush.

JULIA: (*Indicating GORDON.*) Don't take any notice of him. Of course we'll give you an interview.

PATRICK: Thanks. (*To JULIA.*) Are you Kate Donnelly?

JULIA: No. I'm Julia Eden.

PATRICK: I beg your pardon. Sorry. (*To KATE.*) You must be Kate then.

(*KATE nods her head. PATRICK shakes her hand.*)

I met your Father three years ago, just before he died. He was a great man. It was like watching a whirlwind to see him conduct. Like being dragged under by a swirling, kaleidoscopic maelstrom. He ranks alongside Solti for me. Genius, there's no other word for it. (*To the others.*) If I could have Kate and one other, one of the men perhaps.

GORDON: I'll do it. (*Shaking PATRICK's hand.*) Gordon Curran.

PATRICK: Pleased to meet you, Gordon.

JULIA: This is the *Eden* Quartet.

DAVID: You should do it, Julia.

GORDON: He said one of the men.

PATRICK: It doesn't matter. Really… Whoever wants to do it.

DAVID: Why can't we all do it?

PATRICK: Well, it's just… It could sound a real mess if you all started to speak at the same time, that's all. It's easier with one or two.

JULIA: Very well. It's your interview.

PATRICK: Great.

(*PATRICK prepares his recording equipment.*)

(*Testing his recording equipment.*) 1 – 2 – 1 – 2 – (*To KATE and GORDON.*) Just a few simple questions, nothing to worry about. (*Interviewing.*) I'm speaking to Kate Donnelly and Gordon Curran of the Eden Quartet. Kate, am I right in saying this is the Quartet's first visit to Belfast?

KATE: That's right.

PATRICK: Your Mother, I believe, was born just a few miles
    from here…

KATE: Actually, no. My grandparents were from Downpatrick,
    though.

PATRICK: Downpatrick. Do you still have relatives there?

KATE: Probably.

PATRICK: Probably listening to us right now, eh… Your Father,
    of course, the late, great Frank Donnelly and your sister,
    the soloist, Anna Donnelly, have performed in Belfast
    many times. How come the Eden Quartet have never been
    here before?

GORDON: We didn't want to get blown up.

KATE: Gordon…

GORDON: She's frightened the IRA are going to kneecap her
    because her old man hasn't paid up his subs to Sinn Fein.

KATE: (*To PATRICK.*) Sorry.

PATRICK: It's alright, I can erase that.
    (*PATRICK switches off his tape recorder and rewinds.*)

JULIA: I knew it'd be a disaster with those two doing it.

KATE: For Christ's sake, Julia.

JULIA: What?

KATE: You're acting like a five-year-old.

JULIA: Don't be so pathetic.

KATE: It's you that's being pathetic.

JULIA: If only you could hear yourself.

KATE: I don't give a toss about the sodding interview.

JULIA: (*Indicating PATRICK.*) Tell that prat there, not me. If
    he wants to interview you instead of me that's absolutely
    bloody wonderful.
    (*JULIA turns to go.*)

PATRICK: Wait. No… If, er, if you want to do the interview as
    well –

JULIA: No thank you, I've got more important things to do.

DAVID: Julia…
    (*JULIA stops.*)

PATRICK: I'm sorry. I didn't mean to insult you. I think you're
    a great violinist, I was just going for the Irish angle, that's
    all. It'd be a privilege to talk to you.
    (*JULIA exits.*)

DAVID: Julia… (*Exits.*)

PATRICK: Shit.

GORDON: Don't worry about her. She'll be back – As soon as she makes sure you never work again.

KATE: You'd be better off interviewing her. Really…

PATRICK: You think so?

KATE: Yes. I'm not very good at interviews.

PATRICK: Right. It was great meeting you… Right. Bye.

(*PATRICK exits. GORDON opens a bag and takes out a small architect's model of a concert hall made from balsa wood.*)

KATE: What's that?

GORDON: It's a model of this place. I nicked it from the foyer.

KATE: Why?

(*GORDON crosses to JULIA's two violin cases, one of which is open. He lifts a duster off the violin in the open case and takes it out.*)

You better not let Julia see you with her Guadagnini.

GORDON: Don't worry, she won't. Is this the expensive one or the really, really expensive one?

KATE: The really, really expensive one.

GORDON: Good.

(*GORDON puts the violin to one side.*)

KATE: Gordon, for Christ's sake, that violin is worth nearly six hundred thousand pounds.

GORDON: Don't panic.

KATE: What are you going to do?

GORDON: The model is placed in the violin case, like so. The duster is placed over the model, like so. Enter Julia Eden. Gordon Curran trips – Oh no! He stumbles towards her Guadagnini – Oh no! He brings his foot down – Crrrrunch!

KATE: You're such a bastard, Gordon.

GORDON: I know. It's perfect.

KATE: Do me a favour, Gordon… Wait till I get back. I don't want to miss this.

GORDON: My pleasure.

(*KATE exits. GORDON is about to hide JULIA's violin when she re-enters.*)

JULIA: What are you doing with my violin!

GORDON: Is it yours?

JULIA: Give it to me. (*JULIA snatches the violin from him and inspects it.*) Where's Kate?

GORDON: Doing a dirty protest.

(*DAVID re-enters.*)

DAVID: You alright?

(*DAVID and JULIA embrace. GORDON removes the model from JULIA's violin case. They do not see him.*)

JULIA: I hate her.

DAVID: Hey, c'mon. It wasn't Kate's fault.

(*JULIA pulls away from DAVID.*)

JULIA: She did it deliberately.

(*JULIA places the violin back in the case and lays the duster across it.*)

(*To GORDON.*) What were you going to do with my violin?

GORDON: That guy from the radio station offered me twenty quid for it.

(*KATE re-enters.*)

JULIA: (*To KATE.*) You've got a nerve.

KATE: I told him to interview you, didn't he find you?

JULIA: Oh, he found me alright. I told him where to go.

KATE: That was clever.

JULIA: And what's that supposed to mean?

KATE: You've got one hell of an ego problem, do you know that?

JULIA: Really… Is that what you think?

KATE: Yes.

JULIA: You are so bitter and twisted. Kate, I do know what this is all about.

KATE: Oh, do you…

JULIA: Shall I tell you – Self-pity.

KATE: What?

JULIA: Everyone in your family is successful, except you. And you can't stand it.

KATE: Shut up.

JULIA: You can't stand the fact that you'll never be half the musician your sister is.

DAVID: Julia…

(*KATE stands over JULIA's open violin case.*)

KATE: (*To GORDON.*) Did you do it?

GORDON: No, she –

JULIA: You can't stand the fact that you're a nobody.

(*KATE raises her foot.*)

GORDON: No!

(*KATE brings her foot down on the violin and stamps on it repeatedly. GORDON buries his head in his hands, JULIA falls to her knees in disbelief, DAVID stands with mouth and eyes wide open with shock. KATE stops.*)

Oh, no. Oh, no…

KATE: What?

(*JULIA lifts off the duster and holds up the smashed instrument. She dissolves into tears.*)

I didn't know…I didn't.

(*Lights down.*
Interval.)

QUARTET PIECE

THREE : 2

As before. After the Belfast concert. Wine, sandwiches, quiche on the table.
KATE, JULIA, DAVID and GORDON enter with their instruments.

JULIA: (*To KATE.*) That was singularly the worst performance
I've ever heard from you.

KATE: I've got things on my mind.

JULIA: What kind of a ridiculous excuse is that?

KATE: Julia, it was an accident.

JULIA: Oh yes, it looked like it.

GORDON: I told you, it was my fault. Anyway, you'll get the
insurance money.

JULIA: You are such a birdbrain. No amount of money in the
world will ever replace the tone of that instrument.
(*DAVID puts his arms around JULIA.*)

GORDON: I'm going to get some air – You will pay the
ransom, won't you, if the IRA kidnap me?
(*GORDON exits.*)

DAVID: (*To JULIA.*) It's alright. You'll find another violin just
as good. You played really well tonight considering what
happened.

JULIA: 'Considering'! 'Considering'! What's that supposed to
mean?

DAVID: I was just saying –

JULIA: You're trying to tell me I played awfully, aren't you
– That's what 'considering' means!

DAVID: I didn't say that.

JULIA: It's what you meant.

DAVID: No.

JULIA: 'Considering' that woman destroyed one of the finest
violins in the world. 'Considering' I was elbowed out of
an interview. 'Considering' I sounded like a cat on heat
– Everything is absolutely bloody marvellous, wonderful,
couldn't be better.

DAVID: You were good.

JULIA: 'Good'! Don't patronise me!
(*JULIA takes a bottle of herbal tranquillizers from her bag and
takes a tablet.*)

My nerves are absolutely shredded.

(*Suddenly a masked terrorist – GORDON wearing a balaclava – bursts in pointing at them what appears to be a sawn-off shotgun in a carrier bag.*)

GORDON: (*As terrorist. Shouting.*) Down! Get down!

(*DAVID, JULIA and KATE lay on their fronts. DAVID turns round to look at the terrorist.*)

GORDON: (*As terrorist.*) Don't look!

KATE: What –

GORDON: (*As terrorist.*) Shut up!

(*A brief pause, then GORDON removes the balaclava and turns to the audience. He grins, then turns back to the others.*)

You can get up now.

(*They slowly turn around.*)

It was a joke.

(*JULIA bursts into tears. DAVID holds her.*)

KATE: (*Furious.*) You fucking idiot! What the hell do you think you're doing!

GORDON: It was only a joke. I just wanted to cheer you all up.

DAVID: That's it. You know, it's about time someone taught you a lesson.

GORDON: What you going to do? Meditate at me?

(*JULIA is breathing erratically, almost hyperventilating.*)

DAVID: Look what you've done!

GORDON: She never could take a joke.

DAVID: This is not funny.

GORDON: Why don't you go and do some Tai Chi or something.

(*DAVID gives JULIA another herbal tranquilliser.*)

JULIA: You…

GORDON: Yes…

JULIA: You bastard!

GORDON: Well, that was worth waiting for.

JULIA: My Father was in the Paras. He served in Northern Ireland. He was here for three years on and off in the Seventies. He was a colonel for Christ's sake – We lived in constant fear of our lives.

GORDON: I didn't know that. I mean, I knew he was in the army. You never said anything about Ireland.

KATE: He was in Belfast?

JULIA: Belfast, Londonderry, Enniskillen, all over. He was one of the first to come out here in '69. I hate the IRA.

KATE: Someone has to stand up to the British.

JULIA: Nothing is worth murdering for.

KATE: That's not what the British army seem to think.

JULIA: That's a disgusting thing to say. The army are here to protect people.

KATE: They're an occupying force.

JULIA: Spare me the Socilaist Workers' Party rhetoric.

GORDON: You leave the Socialist Workers' Party out of this.

JULIA: (*To KATE.*) Don't you feel any shame?

KATE: Shame? What are you talking about?

JULIA: The things the IRA do.

KATE: The 'things' the IRA do are no worse than the 'things' the Unionist paramilitaries do.

JULIA: Which is precisely why the army have to be here.

KATE: It's an outrage they're here at all.

JULIA: Maybe you're right. Get the troops out. Get the army back to England and let the Irish get on with killing each other.

KATE: When will your sort realise it's about time you stopped playing at Empires.

JULIA: What the hell do you mean, 'my sort'? You were born in London. You were brought up in London.

KATE: So what?

GORDON: No one gives a shit about Ireland anymore, anyway.

KATE: People like you don't give a shit about anything.

GORDON: Pardon me for breathing.

KATE: Just keep out of it.

GORDON: Kate, I couldn't give a toss if you people want to be part of the great Irish potato republic.

DAVID: I think it's wrong to say no one gives a damn about Ireland anymore.

GORDON: Do you?

DAVID: There are a lot of people who think Ireland should be united.

JULIA: David, don't be stupid.

DAVID: It's true.

GORDON: Just make the cheque out to Gerry Adams.

DAVID: I do not give money to the IRA.

(*Enter SECURITY GUARD.*)

SECURITY GUARD: Excuse me, I don't suppose any of you have seen a scale model of the concert hall lying about?

(*They are all silent.*)

No? Ah, well… Oh, just one more thing. Well, two actually. If you see a balaclava and a plastic bag with a thermos in it, I'd be grateful if you could give me a shout. The balaclava's mine, the thermos belongs to my brother. He'll be a right pain if I turn up without it. He's always looking for a reason to have a go at me. Anything, I think it's the only pleasure he gets in life. That and going to Ibrox every now and then.

GORDON: Ibrox? Glasgow Rangers?

SECURITY GUARD: Unless Rangers and Celtic have embarked upon a highly unlikely ground-sharing scheme, then I presume it is Glasgow Rangers we go to watch, yes.

GORDON: Here you go.

(*GORDON hands the SECURITY GUARD the model, carrier bag with flask and balaclava. He then takes the GUARD to one side and whispers something in his ear. The GUARD looks over his shoulder at DAVID, then exits.*)

DAVID: What did you say to him?

GORDON: Nothing.

DAVID: Don't lie. You told him something. You blamed me.

GORDON: No I didn't. Well…

DAVID: What did you say?

GORDON: I explained that you were a kleptomaniac – Don't worry, he won't say nothing. I told him Ian Paisley was your uncle.

DAVID: Thank you, Gordon.

(*DAVID puts his cape on.*)

JULIA: Where are you going?

DAVID: Nowhere. It's freezing in here. I think I'm coming down with something. Flu, a cold or something.

JULIA: Well don't you dare give it to me.

(*DAVID picks up a piece of quiche and takes a bite.*)

DAVID… There's meat in it. Meat. Look. Look, meat. MEAT!!!

(*GORDON takes the quiche from DAVID and inspects it.*)

GORDON: No. You're alright.

DAVID: Oh, thank God. Thank God.

GORDON: It's only bacon.

DAVID: NO!!!

(*DAVID runs off.*)

JULIA: He hasn't eaten meat since he was seven years old.

GORDON: Correction – He hasn't eaten meat since he was
seven years old…until just now.

JULIA: This is awful. He loves animals. This will torture him.
(*To GORDON.*) What have you done?

GORDON: Me? Why do I always get the blame? I didn't kill
the pig. Mind you, (*He takes a bite.*) I've nothing against the
man who did.
(*JULIA exits. KATE sits, she buries her head in her hands.*)
When was the last time you went to confession?

KATE: What?

GORDON: You heard.

KATE: I don't know. Years ago.

GORDON: What's it like?

KATE: Gordon…

GORDON: No, I'm being serious. I'm interested. Honest. I
would've loved it. Did you used to make things up?

KATE: Of course not.

GORDON: I would've. Forgive me Father for I have sinned,
I have had impure thoughts. Christ, I'd never get out the
place.

KATE: Do me a favour, Gordon – Go and be an idiot
somewhere else.

GORDON: Don't be so bloody miserable.

KATE: I've had enough of this. I don't think I can stand this
quartet a minute longer.

GORDON: You'll have me in tears in a minute.
(*JULIA re-enters.*)

JULIA: He's locked himself in the toilet.

GORDON: On my way.
(*GORDON exits. Lighting state changes. Violin music.*)

KATE: (*To audience.*) When Dad died I didn't feel a thing. Anna
couldn't make it to the funeral – too busy.

JULIA: (*As Anna.*) I was in Australia.

KATE: Don't worry, I couldn't have cared less whether you were there or not... You know, the only time Dad ever mentioned Ireland was to slag it off. That's why he didn't want to be buried over here. He was blind to everything apart from himself.

JULIA: (*As Anna.*) That's not true. Why did you hate him so much?

KATE: He shouldn't have played that concert.

JULIA: (*As Anna.*) What concert?

KATE: Bloody Sunday.

JULIA: (*As Anna.*) Christ Kate, we were only children.

KATE: What difference does that make?

JULIA: (*As Anna.*) He was a musician, not a politician or a soldier. He didn't shoot anyone.

KATE: Do you remember when we were at school? You used to pretend you were English.

JULIA: (*As Anna.*) I did not.

KATE: You did. Must be your selective memory at work again. What about when you took all my things and threw them in the dustbin?

JULIA: (*As Anna.*) Children, Kate. Just children.

KATE: You've always wanted me out of the way.

JULIA: (*As Anna.*) This is pure paranoia.

KATE: Is it?

JULIA: (*As Anna.*) You're just being self indulgent.

KATE: Me! Self indulgent! The only time you ever condescend to speak to people is when you want something from them. But we have to be ready to massage your ego at a moment's notice – Yes, you're wonderful, Anna. Oh, but Anna the way you play it is so beautiful. Incredible, Anna. Extraordinary, Anna. Sublime, Anna. The tragedy is you don't even realise you're doing it, that you hurt people when you do the things you do, when you put them down, when you make your demands of them. It hurts. Like it used to hurt me when you gave me that look of yours – that 'play it better' look, that 'I'm better than you' look. Why do we always have to be so careful about what we say and do when you're around? Leave Anna alone, Anna's not in a good mood today. Don't die Kate, you might upset Anna for her performance this evening... The atmosphere changes totally the moment you enter a room, and it's not charisma, it's unease, unease at the fact that you allow no one to act naturally in your prescence, everyone has to submit before the mighty Anna Donnelly.

JULIA: (*As Anna.*) You're jealous.

KATE: No, I'm not jealous, Anna, not any more. I wouldn't want to be you, not for the greatest musical gift in the world.

(*Lighting state returns to normal. GORDON re-enters.*)

GORDON: (*Calling offstage.*) This way, Merlin.

(*DAVID enters.*)

JULIA: David, oh God, you look terrible. Why wouldn't you let me in?

DAVID: It's alright, I've made myself sick.

GORDON: Did I ever tell you about the time I threw up at the fair?

JULIA: Yes. And we don't want to hear it again.

GORDON: I'm going back to the hotel. (*As GORDON turns to go he picks up a packet of crisps.*) Anyone want this bag of smokey bacon crisps?... Suit yourselves.

(*GORDON exits. JULIA sits DAVID down and places her hand on his forehead to feel his temperature.*)

JULIA: Tongue.

DAVID: I'm not dying, Julia.

JULIA: I'm only trying to look after you.

DAVID: Well don't. You know how it aggravates me having people make a fuss when I'm ill.

JULIA: Thank you very much. (*JULIA collects her things.*)

DAVID: Julia.

(*JULIA exits.*)

Shit.

KATE: Hasn't been a very good day, has it...

DAVID: You could say that.

KATE: I've had enough of this quartet, David. I'm thinking of leaving.

DAVID: No. The quartet needs you.

KATE: Are you sure about that?

DAVID: Hey, come here.

(*KATE crosses to DAVID. He holds open his cape, she puts her arms inside and they embrace.*)

Now as I was young and easy under the apple boughs
About the lilting house and happy as the grass was green…
KATE: What's that?
DAVID: Nothing. Just some words that came into my head.
(*Lights down.*)

QUARTET PIECE

FOUR : 1

A dressing room in a concert hall in Cardiff. DAVID is alone. He goes through a short series of tai chi movements then turns to the audience. He has a cold. Altered lighting state.

DAVID: (*To audience.*) You know, I was always convinced there was something from the past calling to me – a voice, some kind of cry for recognition. When I was younger, certain words, a phrase, names, places I'd never even heard of kept coming into my head. I tried not to think about it. But I kept getting these insane, drunken dreams – I mean, dreams about being drunk – And I was only a child, I didn't drink, still don't, not really. But in my dreams I was this mad alcoholic… And there was a woman, we tore the hell out of each other… Mum and Dad sent me for tests, everything. I've been in therapy of one sort or another since I was seven years old, my brother too. Problem with me was, no matter who they sent me to, no matter how much they paid, I just couldn't seem to shake it. Hot sweats, delirium tremens – I tell you, it's no fun waking up with a hangover when all you drank the day before is Ribena. Then, when I was about fourteen, our English teacher told us about a radio play written by this Welsh poet set in a village called Llareggub. I nearly freaked. It was one of the words I'd been hearing in my sleep… Scared the shit out of me. I went straight to the library. *Under Milk Wood* – I learned that play by heart… 'To begin at the beginning: It is spring, moonless night in the small town, starless and bible-black…' Somehow, having a conscious knowledge of the play seemed to cast it out from my unconscious, or it got exorcised, or something, I don't know. Fact is, whatever it was I never really thought about it again for years. But then, about six months ago, the dreams started to come back again, stronger, more vivid than ever. I saw my therapist and he recomended I see a colleague of his – said she might be able to help me; She did. She changed me; my life; everything... See – I discovered that in a past life I'd been Dylan Thomas... (*GORDON enters.*)

GORDON: (*To audience.*) Why is it these places all look the same? (*To DAVID.*) Hey, I've just been to the bar – No one speaks English.

DAVID: The Welsh take a pride in their language.

GORDON: Is that what it is... I thought they all had bronchitis.

DAVID: Being here now... This is like coming home for me.

GORDON: What? Israel?

DAVID: No... This is a special place. I just know I've been here before. It fills me with a sense of power. This country, this city, it's a panacea...a...a lacuna, a portal through which I may at last glimpse the man I once was and, who knows, maybe even the man I am to be.

GORDON: What in Rod Stewart's name are you talking about?

DAVID: Nothing.

GORDON: (*To audience.*) Not going on about Iron John is he?

DAVID: (*To audience.*) You see what I have to put up with? (*To GORDON.*) Just because I try to understand my masculinity.

GORDON: Is that what it's all about then?

DAVID: There's no point in trying to explain it to you. Besides, I'm into past life therapy now.

GORDON: You what?

DAVID: I believe that I have lived before as someone else.

GORDON: So you mean, like, in a past life I could've been Mary Queen of Scots?

DAVID: It's not imposible.

GORDON: I like it. So who were you?

DAVID: No chance.

GORDON: Ah, go on, tell me.

DAVID: And have you go on about it all night? I'm not completely cracked, Gordon.

GORDON: I bet it was Moses.

DAVID: Don't be ridiculous.

GORDON: King Kong?

(*JULIA enters. She slumps down into one of the chairs.*)

JULIA: God, I feel awful. David, have you got my Olbas Oil lozenges?

DAVID: I don't think so.

JULIA: Shit. My throat's killing me. I knew we should never have come.

GORDON: Hey Julia, what's it like sleeping with several men at the same time?

JULIA: What are you insinuating?

DAVID: I told him about the therapy – Not who… Just the therapy.

JULIA: More fool you. (*Sighs.*) This place is so depressing.

DAVID: Give it a chance, Julia. We've only been here a couple of hours. You'll feel better once you're out there and the adrenalin's pumping.

JULIA: Spare me the pearls of wisdom, David. My nose is bunged up, I'm aching all over, my throat's so sore I can hardly swallow… I'm not in the mood to be told I'll feel better later.

DAVID: I've got a cold too, you know.

JULIA: Yes, I do know – you gave it to me.

DAVID: It wasn't deliberate.

JULIA: I feel like death warmed up. What if I'm too ill to play?

DAVID: You'll survive.

JULIA: Did you remember to bring the gelsemium the homeopath prescribed for me?

DAVID: Yes.

(*DAVID hands a small bottle to JULIA, then continues with his tai chi.*)

GORDON: So who does he think he was?

JULIA: That's for him to tell you, not me.

DAVID: (*As he exercises.*) Thank you, Julia.

GORDON: Shut up, Grasshopper. (*To JULIA.*) Tell me. Go on, I won't tell no one else, promise.

JULIA: Don't be so bloody adolescent.

(*JULIA turns away from GORDON.*)

David, do you think there'll be time for us to get to the Psychic Phenomena Conference in Newport tomorrow?

GORDON: Surely you already know that.

JULIA: Don't be so facetious. David?

(*DAVID stops doing his tai chi.*)

DAVID: Julia, can't you see I'm doing my Tai Chi?

(*JULIA is upset. she buries her head in her hands. DAVID crosses to her.*)

Hey, Julia. Come on… Come on.

JULIA: You don't care.

DAVID: Of course I care. I didn't mean to be insensitive.

JULIA: I feel terrible.

DAVID: I know. I know.

JULIA: You can't even be bothered to answer one simple question.

DAVID: I'm sorry. Of course we'll go. I'll make sure there's time. Julia… I love you.

(*JULIA looks at DAVID.*)

Really… You mean so much to me. You're the only woman I ever truly loved.

JULIA: And I love you, David.

GORDON: (*Contemptuously.*) Oh, please…

DAVID: Let's not fall out.

(*DAVID kisses JULIA. They embrace.*)

JULIA: It's my fault. I can be a selfish bitch…

DAVID: No.

GORDON: Yes.

DAVID: Shut up, Gordon. (*To JULIA.*) You know, I think what the therapist said was right, this could be a time of catharsis for me.

GORDON: Moshe Dayan.

DAVID: What?

GORDON: Moshe Dayan – I bet that's who it was. I mean, who you were.

DAVID: What the hell is it with you?

GORDON: I could poke you in the eye if it'd help you get into him a bit more.

(*DAVID stands aggressively in front of GORDON.*)

DAVID: What is this? You get off on anti-semitism now?

JULIA: Will you two stop behaving like such louts.

DAVID: He has to cheapen everything.

GORDON: Alright, alright. Don't get your tallith in a twist.

JULIA: You should never have told him, David.

GORDON: Lend us a fiver and I'll go back to the bar.

JULIA: You shouldn't be drinking.

GORDON: I'm not. I need it for a video game – *Every Second Counts*. It's based on that Paul Daniels TV quiz. Dead good… Don't look at me like that… Well…?

DAVID: Those games are addictive.

GORDON: No they're not. Lend us some money… Go on… Sod you then.

(*GORDON exits.*)

JULIA: I do understand how important this is for you.

DAVID: I know you do.

JULIA: My stepfather was Welsh.

DAVID: Really. You never told me that before.

(*KATE enters – GORDON follows her on.*)

GORDON: Just five quid, Kate.

KATE: I haven't got it.

GORDON: God, I hate you mean bastards.

(*GORDON exits. Lighting state alters.*)

DAVID: Light breaks where no sun shines; Where no sea runs, the waters of the heart Push in their tides… (*To audience.*) See, it just comes to me. Dylan Thomas. God, it makes me dizzy. Words, images – swimming at me. That therapist saved me from drowing in the Lethe. Strange, strange…

(*KATE, as Therapist, moves forward.*)

KATE: (*As Therapist.*) Tell me more.

DAVID: I'm running, a running drunk. I don't even know why I'm in a hurry. My head's light, but my body…my body feels like lead. I can taste the air, the traffic. Pollution…

KATE: (*As Therapist.*) Busy, huh? A city?

DAVID: Maybe. An underground station – I'm running past an underground station into the road, nearly get run over… I'm drinking, smoking. A pub. Laughing, shouting…

KATE: (*As Therapist.*) London?

DAVID: I don't know.

KATE: (*As Therapist.*) Do you know Regent Street?

DAVID: Of course.

KATE: (*As Therapist.*) Langham Place… Portland Place…

DAVID: Portland… Does sound familiar. Portland Place, yes.

KATE: (*As Therapist.*) The BBC.

DAVID: What?

KATE: (*As Therapist.*) Dylan Thornas often worked for the BBC. Broadcasting House, He used to drink at the pubs nearby – Portland Place, Langham Place, Regent Street. Usually, The George.

DAVID: The George… Yes! That's incredible… Incredible!

KATE: (*As Therapist.*) Is there anything else, in your past, your family's past that might link you to Dylan Thomas? Have you ever lived in Wales?

DAVID: No.

KATE: (*As Therapist.*) What about your family? Friends?

DAVID: Wait – Wait! Shit! There is something. My grandparents – In the thirties, when they left Germany. Holy shit! They wanted to get to the States – New York. They paid this merchant sea captain some stupid amount of money and he promised to take them with him the next time he sailed across. Yes… My Grandmother told me about it…

(*JULIA, as DAVID's Grandmother, steps forward.*)

JULIA: (*As Grandmother.*) We were such schmucks – twenty, thirty of us crammed on this tiny boat. Two days later, 'We're here,' he says, 'Welcome to America.' 'If I'd've known it was so close I'd've swum,' I tell him. So we get off the boat in the middle of the night and we end up walking the streets for a week. We find a place to stay and gradually we work up the courage to speak to people. It's then we find out, this isn't New York, it's Cardiff. Six weeks we'd spent looking for the Statue of Liberty in Cardiff.

(*JULIA moves away.*)

DAVID: They never did get to America. Just got as far as Golders Green and then stopped.

(*KATE moves away. GORDON and GARETH enter.*)

GORDON: I want you all to meet Gareth.

GARETH: Don't embarrass me, Gordon.

GORDON: Gareth and I both have something in common… We hate Sir Michael Tippett.

GARETH: I don't hate him, I just don't like his work very much.

JULIA: Do you have to bring your pick-ups back here?

GARETH: Pick-ups?

GORDON: Take no notice, she's got a very strange sense of humour.

GARETH: Oh… I like a bit of off-the-wall humour.

GORDON: Gareth knows all about us.

GARETH: (*Pointing to each in turn.*) Kate Donnelly, David Boam, Julia… Right? I suppose you could call me a bit of a groupie.

DAVID: Listen, we're rather busy right now.

GARETH: Better go then. I don't want to get in the way.

GORDON: No. Stay. I insist.

JULIA: Why don't you both go away and get on with your sordid business somewhere else.

GARETH: (*To GORDON.*) That another one of her jokes, is it?

GORDON: You could say that.

JULIA: Gordon. Out!

GORDON: Come on, Gareth, we know when we're not wanted. (*Singing 'Do you think I'm sexy?' by Rod Stewart to himself as he goes.*) 'If you want my body, and you think I'm sexy, come on baby let me know…'
(*GARETH and GORDON exit. KATE laughs to herself.*)

JULIA: (*To KATE.*) What are you sniggering at?

KATE: Nothing… Nothing.

JULIA: Just you thank your lucky stars I'm well enough to go on tonight. Wouldn't want a repeat of our last Purcell Room concert, would we, Kate? Do you remember? I had appendicitis, remember Kate? You had to take over from me. Do you remember all those people who asked for their money back when they heard I wasn't playing?

KATE: Why do you always have to bring that up?

JULIA: Because it amuses me.

KATE: They assumed the concert had been cancelled. They were content enough when they heard the quartet were still playing.

JULIA: They asked for their money back.

DAVID: Come on you two, this is getting us nowhere.

JULIA: Trust you to take her side.

DAVID: I'm not taking sides.
(*JULIA exits.*)
She's in a bad mood.

KATE: She's always in a bad mood.

DAVID: You alright, haven't got this virus have you?

KATE: No. David, I've arranged a couple of auditions for after the London concert.

DAVID: You don't hang about... Is there nothing I can say to persuade you –

KATE: No... Christ, I hate auditions. I get so nervous.

DAVID: You'll be alright. I remember when you auditioned for us – you were great.

KATE: Pity I never lived up to it.

DAVID: Don't put yourself down all the time. Hey, my cello teacher once told me a story about a Jewish friend of his in the war. About how this friend had to to audition Jews for an orchestra in one of the death camps. He knew he was sentencing all the musicians he didn't choose to death. Men and women, literally playing for their lives.

KATE: You already told me that story before.

DAVID: Did I? I always forget who I've told what to. You know, sometimes – when I'm talking to someone I hear a voice in my head telling me I've already said this to them before – it's so embarrassing, I get paranoid they must think I'm a real idiot... Kate, about Belfast –

KATE: I don't want to talk about it.

DAVID: Don't be like that.

KATE: I don't want to talk about it.

DAVID: God, I hate myself sometimes.

KATE: What's this – Seduction by self-pity?

(*JULIA enters. She crosses aggressively and sits down in tight-lipped fury.*)

DAVID: Julia... Julia, what is it?

JULIA: Twelve tickets. They've sold twelve sodding tickets for tonight.

DAVID: We're not that well known in Wales.

JULIA: Obviously!

(*Lights down.*)

QUARTET PIECE

FOUR : 2

As before. After the Cardiff concert. JULIA watches as DAVID pours himself a glass of wine. He is smoking a cigarette.

JULIA: What are you trying to prove?

DAVID: If I am him, I have to drink and smoke like him.

JULIA: Dylan Thomas didn't drink Chardonnay.

DAVID: How do you know? Besides this is only my second glass, I'm not about to run naked through the streets of Cardiff reciting *Under Milk Wood.*

JULIA: I can't work with Gordon any more, David... David, are you listening to me?

DAVID: Yes, yes. I'm listening.

JULIA: He's a liability.

DAVID: Kate's just going through a bad time.

JULIA: I'm not talking about Kate... You've already told me she wants to leave. No, it's Gordon. Gordon's got to go.

DAVID: Gordon?... Alright. If you want him out, he's out.

JULIA: I know it's the right thing to do. I've consulted the runes. Give my shoulders a rub will you.

(Before DAVID can begin to massage JULIA's shoulder GORDON and KATE enter.)

GORDON: *(To DAVID.)* What're you doing?

DAVID: What does it look like? I'm smoking a cigarette and drinking a glass of wine.

GORDON: But you don't smoke, you don't drink – Well, one can of piss-weak lager every time the Green Party win an election, maybe.

DAVID: What do you call a thousand violas at the bottom of the sea?

GORDON: Eh?

DAVID: A start... What's the difference between a viola and a trampoline? – You don't have to take your shoes and socks off to jump up and down on a viola.

GORDON: My God, he's telling jokes.

DAVID: I'm just being myself for once, that's all.

(DAVID exits.)

JULIA: David... My massage...

(*JULIA looks at GORDON, then exits.*)

KATE: Where's Gareth?

GORDON: He'll be here later.

KATE: You better not let Julia catch you two up to your 'sordid' business.

GORDON: Actually it's Julia that Gareth has the sordid business with, not me. He's the new marketing director for Balls Brothers soft drinks company.

KATE: What?

GORDON: Our sponsors. Remember?

KATE: Why didn't you say something?

GORDON: She didn't give me the chance.

KATE: She'll be furious.

GORDON: I know. Great, isn't it. And guess what – He fancies her.

KATE: No…

GORDON: Yes. Some people are very peculiar… Hey, has David mentioned anything about past life therapy to you?

KATE: A bit.

GORDON: Did he say anything about who he was?

KATE: No.

GORDON: You're lying. Tell me.

KATE: I don't know.

GORDON: Tell me.

KATE: Honestly, Gordon. I haven't got a clue.

GORDON: I'll find out. Tell you what, we'll do twenty questions? No, that game – what's it called? Botticelli… What letter does it begin with?

(*DAVID re-enters.*)

DAVID: My ears are burning, not talking about me are you?

(*JULIA re-enters.*)

KATE: Julia, I won't be driving back to London with you and David in the morning. I'm going to get the train back tonight.

JULIA: Got a man stashed away at last, have you?

KATE: No, Julia. There's no man.

JULIA: People are beginning to talk about you, you know.

KATE: What do you mean?

JULIA: You know full well what I mean. How long is it since you last had a relationship?

KATE: I don't see what the hell that's got to do with you.

JULIA: You should get yourself a man, Kate. It reflects badly on all of us.

KATE: It's got nothing to do with you.

JULIA: It has plenty to do with me. You haven't been out with a man all the time I've known you. Now, I don't care if you are a bit the other way, but I don't want people making suggestions about me.

KATE: I'm not a lesbian – Just because I'm not running around desperate to give a blow job to one of the Chippendales.

JULIA: Don't be so crude.

KATE: Listen, I'm very happy as I am, thank you. I don't need a man. And I have absolutely no intention of getting tied down, married off, or up the junction. There are more important things. I enjoy being me, there's no time for men. Besides, I have to concentrate on my playing.

JULIA: We all know that, Kate.

KATE: You cow!

JULIA: Anyway, it's small wonder people think you're a dyke the way you dress.

KATE: What's wrong with the way I dress?

JULIA: Jeans and T-shirts.

KATE: God, give me strength… I am not a dyke. I am not celibate. I just don't go around shouting about it.

JULIA: Oh, so all of a sudden you're Mata Hari, are you?

KATE: Believe it or not, Julia, I do fuck. I fuck men.

JULIA: Really?

KATE: Yes, really.

JULIA: In your dreams, maybe.

KATE: Perhaps you should ask David about it.

(*Pause.*)

JULIA: What?

KATE: Nothing.

JULIA: What did you say? David…

DAVID: Don't look at me, I don't know what she's talking about.

JULIA: (*To KATE.*) Explain yourself… Explain yourself!!!

KATE: There's nothing to explain.

JULIA: (*To DAVID.*) What's she talking about? Tell me!!!

DAVID: Tell you what?

JULIA: Did you… Did you – with her.

DAVID: Don't be ridiculous.

JULIA: I'll know if you're lying. I can tell if you're lying. I'll find out, David. Look me in the eye… Look me in the eye! Swear to me you don't know what she's talking about.

DAVID: You're mad.

JULIA: Swear… Look at me! Swear it.

DAVID: I swear. Now can we forget all this.

JULIA: Why have you gone red?

DAVID: I haven't gone red.

JULIA: You're as red as a sodding double decker bus!

DAVID: Jesus!

GORDON: I thought you didn't believe in Jesus.

JULIA: David, I want the truth. The truth. David…

DAVID: It was nothing.

JULIA: What was nothing? What was it? Where?

DAVID: In Belfast.

JULIA: You slept with her?

DAVID: It was only a one night stand.

JULIA: You made love to her?

DAVID: I didn't enjoy it.

KATE: Nor did I.

DAVID: That wasn't what you said at the time.

KATE: I didn't want to offend your fragile ego, David.

DAVID: Frigid bitch.

KATE: Well, you're not exactly Captain Fantastic.

JULIA: How could you do this to me, David? How could you do it?

DAVID: It's her, she's a cock teaser.

KATE: What!

JULIA: (*To KATE.*) Why do you want to split us up?

KATE: I don't. Christ, I wouldn't want to end up with a prick like him.

DAVID: And I love you, Kate.

GORDON: David…

DAVID: What?

GORDON: You and Julia, you've been sleeping together for some time now, right?

DAVID: Yes.

GORDON: And when we were in Belfast last week you had sex with Kate?

DAVID: Yes.

GORDON: So is it my turn next?

JULIA: How could you do this to me, David? How could you do it?

DAVID: It wasn't my fault.

JULIA: What! Whose fault was it then, Dylan Thomas's? I suppose your past life just crept up on you and told you to jump into bed with every tart you could find.
(*KATE exits.*)

GORDON: Dylan Thomas? He thinks he's Dylan Thomas? (*He laughs.*) Dylan Thomas.

DAVID: Don't take the piss, Gordon. I'm not in the mood.

GORDON: But Dylan Thomas is Welsh.

DAVID: It makes no difference.

GORDON: My God. Next you'll be telling me Cardiff Arms Park is your spiritual home.

DAVID: What are you talking about?

GORDON: Cardiff Arms Park – Rugby. You do know about rugby, don't you?

DAVID: Of course I do.

GORDON: What's a maul?

DAVID: A what?

GORDON: How many points for a try?… A drop goal? You don't know, do you… I thought you were meant to be Welsh.

DAVID: Why don't you shut up.

GORDON: So when do you start drinking Brains Bitter and singing in male voice choirs?
(*DAVID points a threatening finger at GORDON.*)
Come on then, give me your best shot – Bash me with a leak. Poke me in the eye with a daffodil.
(*DAVID Swings a punch at GORDON. GORDON ducks out of the way.*)
Come on then, Barry John.
(*DAVID lines up another punch, then drops his fist and exits.*)
(*Welsh accent.*) There's lovely… (*In his normal voice.*) I'm off to find Kate, tell her she's been sleeping with the Dead Poets Society.

(*GORDON exits. JULIA collects her things together. GARETH enters.*)

GARETH: Do you realise, I must have listened to every single one of your recordings over the past week.

JULIA: What do you want?

GARETH: Thought we might get to know each other. We could go out for a meal, I know a nice place up by Cardiff castle.

JULIA: I don't think so.

GARETH: I'm a great admirer, you know.

JULIA: (*Uninterested.*) Really.

GARETH: On an artistic level as well as – You're very beautiful.

JULIA: And you're very ugly. Now, be a good boy and go lay down in a gutter somewhere.

GARETH: There's no need to be like that.

JULIA: You disgust me.

GARETH: I was only trying to be friendly.

(*DAVID re-enters. GARETH exits.*)

DAVID: Forgive me, Julia.

JULIA: Forgive you... Forgive you! You've got a nerve. I'd be grateful if you moved to a different hotel for tonight. We can talk about things tomorrow. I don't think I want to go to the Newport conference with you.

DAVID: I couldn't have gone anyway.

JULIA: What do you mean?

DAVID: I'm going on a sword forging weekend with my men's group in Abergavenny.

JULIA: Well thank you for telling me, David.

DAVID: I meant to say something earlier... It's been arranged for ages... I'm sorry, Julia... Sorry...

(*JULIA exits. Lighting state alters. Fade up singing of a male voice choir.*)

(*Quoting from Dylan Thomas's 'After the Funeral'.*)

'After the funeral, mule praises, brays,

Windshake of sailshaped ears, muffle-toed tap

Tap happily of one peg in the thi...' Shut up!

(*The male voice choir suddenly stops.*)

'Tap happily of one peg in the thick...in the thick...' Can't remember it. (*He sighs.*) I can't remember it.

(*Lights down.*)

QUARTET PIECE

FIVE : 1

A dressing room in a concert hall in London. GORDON and KATE are standing together. JULIA sits apart from them clutching a piece of paper. There is the intermittent sound of a pneumatic drill somewhere in the distance.

JULIA: Why didn't you tell me, Gordon?

GORDON: You didn't ask.

JULIA: You could've told him I was ill, dying, anything – having a breakdown.

GORDON: I didn't see him again after the concert.

JULIA: You did this deliberately.

GORDON: No, I didn't. It was sheer good fortune.

JULIA: Do you know how much time and effort David and I put into trying to secure this sponsorship deal?

GORDON: It's not my fault. You were the one who called him ugly – Look, it says so in the letter.

KATE: Does David know?

JULIA: Yes. He's furious with you, Gordon.

GORDON: Hell hath no fury like a man in past life therapy. Where is he, anyway?

JULIA: David's not very well. He's had a bit of an accident. But don't tell him I told you. And don't you dare mention anything about it when he comes in. He's already in a state, I don't want him getting any worse. This is an extremely important concert. We may have lost Balls Brothers, but there are other sponsors – perhaps there'll be one out there tonight. Anyway, the Arts Council people are in, if we screw up our grant we really are in trouble… Christ, can't they shut that bloody drill up. What the hell are they doing out there?

GORDON: They're building a new underpass for London's homeless.

KATE: It's something to do with a gas main.

JULIA: Oh wonderful, we're all going to get blown up. Mind you, probably wouldn't be a bad thing, the South Bank's an architectural nightmare.

GORDON: I'm going to tell Melvyn Bragg you said that.

JULIA: (*Placing a hand on her forehead.*) I'm going to have one of my heads, I know I am... It's no good – I can't stand this noise a minute longer. You'll have to go and tell them to stop it.

GORDON: Me? No chance.

(*DAVID enters. One of his legs is in a plaster cast. He has one crutch and is carrying his cello. GORDON and KATE stare at him.*)

How –

DAVID: I don't want to talk about it.

GORDON: Did an anvil fall on your foot?

DAVID: I'm warning you...

JULIA: Go and tell them to stop the drilling, David.

DAVID: Julia, come on. I only just got here. Do you have any idea what it's like trying to get round this giant concrete urinal on one leg.

JULIA: Please.

DAVID: No.

GORDON: The worm has turned.

DAVID: Perhaps later.

GORDON: Almost.

DAVID: I have to practise.

JULIA: Not in here, David, I've got a headache.

DAVID: I'll go and sit ouside, shall I – Freeze my balls off playing to drop-outs.

(*DAVID turns to go. GORDON offers DAVID some money.*)

What's that for?

GORDON: Get you started – You're going busking aren't you?

DAVID: No Gordon, I am not going busking.

GORDON: Give it to one of the dossers then.

DAVID: I am going to practise in the corridor, seeing as I'm not allowed to practise in here. But I will take your money since the walk from the tube station cost me four pounds fifty in hand-outs and copies of *The Big Issue.*

JULIA: David, you are a fool. Why do you give those people money?

GORDON: Why shouldn't he?

JULIA: Because I don't see why decent people should be harrassed into subsidising drug-taking and vagrancy. They're worse than immigrants.

GORDON: Can I borrow your copy of *Mein Kampf* when you've finished with it.

(*GORDON picks up a copy of the* Guardian *(bought on the day of the production) and starts reading. As DAVID turns to exit JAMES enters. He is carrying a tray with a cloth over it.*)

JAMES: Hello, James Thoroughgood. Absolutely terrific to have you here. Big fan. (*He puts the tray down.*) Got some absolutely marvellous news. Royalty in tonight. Don't know who just yet, I've only just heard – But rumour is, it might be… (*He flaps his hands by his ears to indicate a member of the royal family with big ears.*)

JULIA: Charles?

JAMES: (*Putting finger to lip.*) Sssssshhhhh…

DAVID: Are you serious?

JAMES: Absolutely.

(*JULIA grips DAVID's hand.*)

DAVID: (*Sternly.*) Gordon…

GORDON: What?

JULIA: (*To JAMES.*) You are telling the truth, aren't you?

JAMES: Absolutely. Is there a problem?

JULIA: No, no. Please, don't take it the wrong way. We're thrilled.

DAVID: It's a real privilege.

GORDON: I hate –

JULIA: Gordon!

DAVID: So, will we be introduced?

JAMES: Absolutely. Something will be arranged for after the concert… Oh, before I forget. Got a treat for you. Courtesy of Langan's – they're doing the royal buffet. (*He takes the cloth off the tray.*) Oysters! Absolutely gorgeous…

GORDON: Aphrodisiac, eh? Is Charlie-boy bringing Camilla Parker-Bowles?

JULIA: Shut up, Gordon!

GORDON: You better not let David near them or none of us'll be safe… But I forgot, you two don't eat fish… Shame.

JAMES: Oh well, *c'est la vie.*

(*JAMES exits with tray.*)

GORDON: No wait… Damn.

JULIA: This is fantastic.

KATE: Shit!

JULIA: What is it?

KATE: I've forgotten my clothes.

JULIA: You can't go on dressed like like that.

KATE: I'll have to.

JULIA: You can wear my spare dress.

KATE: No chance.

JULIA: What do you mean?

KATE: I'm not wearing one of your frumpish things.

JULIA: Frumpish! My clothes are a damn sight classier than the rags you walk around in. No, I'm sorry Kate, you will wear my dress. (*Pushing a dress at her.*) Here…

DAVID: This is so exciting.

JULIA: Absolutely.

GORDON: God, listen to her she even sounds like him.

JULIA: Don't start, Gordon.

GORDON: The royal family are a bunch of arseholes.

JULIA: Well, Gordon, I must say that's the most potent republican arguement I've heard in a very long time.

DAVID: I really had better get some practice in now.
    (*DAVID exits.*)

GORDON: They're a waste of money.

JULIA: They're this county's greatest asset.

KATE: Asset… Do me a favour – Sarah Ferguson an asset?

JULIA: Sarah Ferguson is not a member of the royal family.

KATE: Of course she is.

JULIA: No she isn't. Not any more.

GORDON: You're off your head.

JULIA: Gordon, why don't you do something useful for once in your life – like going out and telling those gas people to stop that drilling.

GORDON: You go.

JULIA: I can't. My back's murder.

GORDON: Your back? Since when?

JULIA: Since we started these concerts. It's been getting worse and worse. It's a physical reaction to stress.

GORDON: (*Uninterested.*) Really.

JULIA: Kate –

KATE: I've got things to do, Julia.

JULIA: (*Stretching her back.*) It might have something to do with when I fell off my pony.

(*GORDON and KATE ignore her. Pause.*)

I need a herbal infusion.

GORDON: You need a frontal lobotomy.

JULIA: Thank you, Gordon.

GORDON: No problem. (*Returning his attention to the newspaper – he quotes from a sports article or result printed on the day of the performance, if possible relating to Scottish football. Example as follows.*) Forty-one, you believe that? Forty-one goals Ally McCoist's scored for Rangers so far this season.

(*JULIA and KATE ignore him. GORDON turns to a different page. DAVID re-enters, he takes some Lipsil from his bag and puts it on his lips.*)

GORDON: I think I prefer the pink.

DAVID: My lips are chapped.

GORDON: That's what they all say.

(*GORDON continues reading his newspaper.*)

JULIA: David, will you go and have a word with the workmen now?

DAVID: Julia, please... It's really not my repertoire to confront men with pneumatic drills about the noise they're making.

GORDON: Listen to this... (*Paraphrasing from a newspaper article relating to Serbia / Bosnia or another relevant issue pertaining to the break-up of a nation printed on the day of the performance. If the piece of news chosen is not about Serbia / Bosnia the dialogue that follows should be adapted to fit the news item being discussed as necessary. Example as follows.*) Two families in Bosnia, lived next door to each other for years, used to go round to each other's flat for dinner. Muslim family got thrown out, went off wandering the streets and one of the sons got blown to pieces by a mortar. They put the blame for everything that'd happened on their Serbian neighbours, went round, dragged them out of their beds and hung them from the balcony of their flat... Serbs, Croats, Bosnians – They're all mad.

KATE: That's a stupid thing to say, Gordon.

GORDON: Yugoslavia was fine under Tito.

DAVID: You mean communism.

GORDON: What if I do?

KATE: They're fighting for some sense of identity. It's the same here.

GORDON: Britain isn't Yugoslavia.

DAVID: More's the pity. Parts of the British Isles could do with some ethnic cleansing. Get rid of the Scots for a start.

GORDON: Piss off, Taffy.

KATE: You can't stop people being proud of their country – I am.

GORDON: You! Ireland! Christ, you've only ever been there once. And that was a disaster.

JULIA: You're such a hypocrite, Kate.

KATE: I am not a hypocrite.

JULIA: You don't care about Ireland.

KATE: I do. How would you like it if someone drew a line through the middle of England and said anywhere north of Birmingham was another country.

JULIA: Personally speaking, I think it'd be a marvellous idea.

KATE: God, you are so arrogant.

JULIA: (*Patronizing.*) And you're so oppressed, aren't you, darling? You've had such a tough life.

KATE: Actually, Julia, other people apart from you do have problems.

JULIA: I suppose the Irish and the Scottish do have one redeeming feature – At least they're not Welsh.

DAVID: What's that supposed to mean? Anyhow, you're half Welsh.

JULIA: My step-father is Welsh, David. That's a slightly different thing.

DAVID: The Welsh are great.

JULIA: They're vile.

DAVID: You can't base an opinion of an entire nation on one single person.

JULIA: Why not?

(*DAVID exits.*)

GORDON: (*To JULIA.*) So when is it you two are getting married?

JULIA: We're not getting married, Gordon.

GORDON: Oh no. And there was me waiting on tenterhooks for David to ask me to be his best man. I was so looking forward to it – Do you Julia Eden take this man David Dylan Thomas J P R Williams Neil Kinnock Ian Rush Richard Burton Boam to be your lawful wedded Welshman?

(*JULIA stares out at the audience, she is not listening to GORDON. We hear the sound of a cello as DAVID begins practising outside. Lighting state changes. During the following section the sound of the drill gets progressively louder. The cello is superseded by a violin which begins to play a familiar piece of English music.*)

JULIA: (*To audience.*) In the fifties the British held nuclear tests in Australia. My father was part of an observation team. Ten years ago he died in a military hospital in Dorset from an 'unknown' illness. He'd been unwell for months. We all knew it was cancer, but no one dared say anything. No questions – No lies… Things between Mother and Father had been awful for years. They were already divorced when he died… We lived all over the place, that was why it seemed sensible to send me to a boarding school, I didn't mind, it was better than home… Mother pretended she wanted me to be a great success as a violinist, but always hated it when I actually achieved anything. During the holidays she used to ignore me all day then make up transparent excuses to get out of the house at night…

(*KATE, as JULIA's Mother moves forward.*)

KATE: (*As JULIA's Mother.*) Darling, Mummy's got to go to your Aunt Pippa's to make some arrangements for the gymkhana next week.

JULIA: If I ever said anything she just used to shout at me. (*To KATE.*) There isn't a gymkhana next week.

KATE: (*As JULIA's Mother.*) Don't answer me back!

JULIA: It started when Father was in Ireland. Before that, Mother used to go with him on all his postings – Cyprus, Belize… I didn't have any brothers or sisters, so I ended up on my own a lot of the time when I was at home. She started bringing a man back to the house – it went on for years. I knew him as Long John Silver, not because he had a wooden leg or an eye-patch or a parrott, but because he always called me treasure.

(*GORDON, as Long John, moves forward. He pats JULIA on the head.*)

GORDON: (*As Long John. Welsh accent.*) Hello treasure.

JULIA: I hated it.

GORDON: (*As Long John.*) Where's your Mum?

(*GORDON, as Long John, crosses to KATE, as Mother, they caress.*)

JULIA: She used to sneak him in some nights, after I'd gone to bed. They'd be downstairs, talking, laughing. Then, after a while, they'd come upstairs together as discreetly as their drunkenness would allow. They had to come past my door. I used to lay awake listening for them. Then they'd go into the bedroom. I could hear them through the... (*Pause.*) She sent me to hospital because I refused to eat. I felt guilty, like it was my fault. I hated myself, had to punish myself. I'd destroyed everything, I couldn't bear to look at myself, I was repulsive. All the time it kept going through my mind – they would've been happy if I hadn't been born. I felt unconnected, like there was nothing there, like I was floating, already dead, then, these noises, like machines, like animals, music, such strange music in my head.

(*The music begins to warp. The drill has almost reached a crescendo.*)

And voices, familiar voices, voices I'd never heard...

KATE: (*As JULIA's Mother.*) Don't answer me back!

GORDON: (*As Long John.*) Where's your Mum.

(*Pre-recorded voices, music, and drilling now build to a final peak. JULIA covers her ears. DAVID enters.*)

DAVID: Julia, are you alright?

(*DAVID puts his hand on JULIA's shoulder. A sudden cut back to the present. Lighting state returns to normal. Silence. The drill has stopped.*)

Julia, you...

JULIA: I can't do anything about it – I hear myself saying things and I detest myself for it. But I just can't seem to stop it...

DAVID: What's wrong? What is it?

(*JULIA picks up her violin and exits.*)

What's been going on here?

GORDON: A despot in confusion may appear quite the opposite.

DAVID: What?

GORDON: Three across. Nine letters. *Guardian* crossword, David. Or don't they get crosswords in the valleys yet?

(*JAMES enters.*)

JAMES: You're on in about two minutes, okay.

(*DAVID exits.*)

See you out there... I'll do a bit of a spiel first... Break a string. Ha, ha...

(*JAMES turns to go, GORDON stops him.*)

GORDON: Haven't I seen you somewhere before?

JAMES: It's a possibility.

GORDON: How come you always speak with an Irish accent?

JAMES: Apparently, I'm a symbol of the Irish question preying on the British consciousness.

(*GORDON thinks for a moment.*)

GORDON: Bollocks to that!

JAMES: (*To audience.*) Precisely.

(*JAMES exits. KATE puts JULIA's dress on over her T-shirt and jeans.*)

GORDON: Oh, lovely.

KATE: Shut up.

GORDON: You look just like Anne of Green Gables.

KATE: It's not funny, Gordon.

GORDON: You three are such boring bastards.

KATE: Gordon, why do you stay in this quartet if you hate everyone so much?

GORDON: I don't hate everyone. I just don't...'like' anyone.

KATE: You should leave.

GORDON: No. Truth is, I'm happy enough, professionally speaking. Julia's made a name for herself, I admire that – Don't tell her I said so. David's alright. Mind you, they could do with a few less catholics...

KATE: Well, you might just get your wish there.

GORDON: Just a joke, Kate... See, I look upon this quartet as a vehicle to future megastardom.

KATE: If you don't jump, you're in serious danger of being pushed, Gordon.

GORDON: No, they won't do nothing. They might hate my guts, but they know when they're on to a good thing.

KATE: Gordon, Julia and David have been auditioning viola players today.

GORDON: What!... This is a wind-up, right?

KATE: No, Gordon. Why don't you spare yourself the humiliation and say you're leaving after tonight.

GORDON: I'll kill them.

KATE: You should just tell them you've had enough.

GORDON: Don't tell me what to do! How do you know about this?

KATE: Julia told me.

GORDON: So you're in on it as well?

KATE: No.

GORDON: It's alright for you, you Irish slag!

KATE: Don't you call me a slag!

GORDON: Nice little *ménage à trois* you've got going. I thought I was meant to be the pervert. What about the little question of infidelity – Why doesn't she get rid of Dylan Thomas?

KATE: They've sorted out their differences.

GORDON: Sorted out –

KATE: They're going to split up, on a personal level. But stay together professionally.

(*GORDON advances on KATE menacingly. KATE backs away.*)

Gordon... No, Gordon.

GORDON: So it's bye-bye, Gordon.

KATE: It's nothing to do with me. They'll be in breach of contract if they don't continue to work together. It's their quartet, not ours. Gordon... It's not my fault.

GORDON: Come here...

KATE: They might change their minds, Gordon. None of the musicians they auditioned this morning were suitable... Gordon...

(*GORDON lunges at KATE, she grabs a glass of wine and throws the contents at GORDON, it soaks the crotch of his trousers. KATE grabs her violin and exits. GORDON stands motionless for a moment. He picks up his viola and exits. A stage manager positions four chairs, centre forestage then exits. JAMES enters onto forestage.*)

JAMES: We're very privileged to have with us tonight the Eden Quartet... Er... (*He takes a scrap of paper from his pocket and glances at it.*) Over the past few years the Eden Quartet have established a reputation as one of Britain's leading string quartets and their many diverse recordings, from Beethoven to Bartok; Schubert to Schnittke, have met with worldwide acclaim. (*He glances offstage.*) … This evening's concert is the last in a series that has taken the quartet around Britain performing the work of composers native to England, Scotland, Ireland and Wales. (*He glances offstage.*) Ladies and Gentlemen, the Eden Quartet. (*He applauds.*) (*JAMES exits. Enter JULIA, DAVID, KATE and GORDON with instruments. They cross to their seats, acknowledge the audience, then sit. We hear a couple of notes as the musicians check their tuning. House lights down. There is a brief pause, a reverential silence, then JULIA, as leader of the quartet, ensures she has the musicians' attention before counting them in. The instant before the first note is to be played GORDON stands and starts to walk off stage.*)

JULIA: Gordon!… (*Under her breath.*) Shit! (*Calling out.*) Gordon! (*GORDON stops. Blackout.*)
(*The End.*)

INTERNATIONAL CAFÉ
A One Person One Act Play
For performance in restaurants, cafés and bars

Characters

BRIAN
A Scottish Restauranteur

SALVATORE
A Swiss-Italian Chef

AMOS
A Nigerian Waiter

MARGARET
A Londoner

JESUS
A Brazilian Kitchen Assistant

PATRICIA
A US Academic

CLAIRE
A Food & Drink Critic

ANDRIS
A Latvian Dishwasherupper

Note: Dates and names should be updated in accordance with the date of the performance

International Café was first performed at The Supreme Restaurant, London SW11, on 8th November 1998 with the following cast:

Performer, Rupert Degas

Director, Richard Shannon

Producer, Nick Eisen (Chamber Theatre)

(A restaurant. BRIAN enters. BRIAN is an overweight, Scottish restauranteur in his forties.)

BRIAN: Good evening, my name is Brian McLeish. I am the proprietor of the International Café. Bit of a dream, really, this, for me. All came from an idea I had a few years ago when I'd just eaten an onion bhaji and fancied some gnocchi to follow. Suddenly it hit me. You know, the best food from nations all around the world all under one roof. Where you can begin your evenings on the shores of the Danube with a Hungarian Salata, travel to the Atlas Mountains for Moroccan Casserole, and finish up on Broadway with Uncle Sam's delicious Creamy Candies. House rule: No two consecutive courses from the same country. So I borrowed a frightening amount of money from the bank and it was all systems go. Three weeks after opening we got a to-die-for review in *The Guardian*...and it took off. Simple as that. But then it all started to go horribly wrong. See, problem was, for me, this wasn't so much a restaurant as aversion therapy. I used to weigh in at over 26 stone. True. I've got the photos to prove it. You ask Maggie, my wife. She'll be in later. Yes, 26 stone. Pair of trousers you could hold a wedding reception in. Love my food. Thing is, once I start I can't stop. I binge. We all do, I think, if we're honest. Only, when I binge it's not half a dozen Mister Kipling's Cherry Bakewells or a family pack of Cheese Doritos, oh no, it's everything edible within a fifty yard radius. I'm not kidding. And I'm not the kind of binge eater who sits there feeling guilty after a session, wondering why I did it. No no. None of that, 'Oh why did I have to eat the whole loaf' or 'Why did I have to finish the entire tub of St Michael's Lemon Sorbet' nonsense. No no no. With me it's, 'I'm sure Kelloggs are making these boxes smaller,' or 'I'm convinced these family packs of mini Snickers used to have more than just forty-two bars in'. And there is no way I want to make myself sick. No chance of that. Eating stimulates my appetite. The more I eat, the hungrier I get. There's a medical term for it – greedy bastard. And when I go on these binges, it's not 24 hours, it's not a week. No, that'd be too simple. No, when I binge it lasts for between three and five years. I'd been on a four and a half year bender when my therapist suggested I open a restaurant so I could face my demons. Prove I could be around it, without eating it. That's what this place was all about. And it worked, for a while. For sixteen months I existed on a diet of museli, live yoghurt and shaved carrots while my restaurant served some of the most exotic and delicious food in Britain. I slimmed down to thirteen stone. Thirteen stone. It was not easy. We'd been open just over a year and everything was hunky dory…when it happened. One evening, just after we'd closed and the staff had gone home I noticed Chef had left the parmesan out and I thought, ach hell, I'll just grate a wee bit to have with my carrot. I didn't stop eating until about half past nine the following morning. And I only stopped then because I couldn't be bothered to wait for the Chicken Kievs to defrost. I ran to the newsagents across the road and bought the confectionery counter. It cost me three hundred and twelve quid. I couldn't stop. Soon customers were being turned away because we'd nothing left for them to eat. In two months I was back up to twenty-one stone, the restaurant was going under and the only person eating here was me. Then the bank started to call in the loans and I had to lay off the staff. I didn't know what to do. I was already comfort eating for an army. Then one evening my ex-Chef dropped by and we had a chat about the old days. Had a real laugh. See, some of the dishes weren't exactly what you'd call 'kosher'. The Venezuelan glowsnake, for example – jellied eels. Anyway, we were chatting into the early hours, when all of a sudden I realise, it's half past two in the morning, I haven't eaten a thing for over four hours. Hey, says Salvatore, that's my Chef, perhaps that's the answer. Don't eat it, talk about it. So that's what I decided to do. I got the staff back together and…here we are. Ladies and Gentlemen welcome to the International Café. Where you can gorge yourself on story food from around the world. Story food from Africa to South America; from Latvia to Lavender Hill. Story food brought to you by the people who prepare and serve it. Tonight's guest lecture will be delivered by Dr Patricia Margoles of the University of Michigan and there will also be special guest appearance by *Guardian* Food and Drink critic Claire Broom. Chef, Salvatore Maldini, will be round with starters shortly. I should warn you that, well, like all the best chefs, Salvatore is a bit temperamental. He can get a tad...violent. So don't upset him. He drinks. But please don't say anything. Oh, and he's a compulsive liar. Enjoy your meal.

(*BRIAN exits. SALVATORE enters. SALVATORE is a heavy drinking Swiss-Italian chef in his late fifties. He swigs from a bottle of cooking sherry. He has a meat cleaver which he slams down into a breadboard every now and then to punctuate his story.*)

SALVATORE: You remember 1966? I play in the World Cup, you know that! Me! Centre half. Centre back they call it now. Salvatore Maldini. You hear of Paolo Maldini? No, I am not him. I am Salvatore Maldini. You hear of Cesare Maldini? No, not him. I am Salvatore Maldini. He is the man. You know that John Terry? Wanker! Rio Ferdinand. Wanker! Senderos... He is very good. I like the Arsenal. But he is not as good as Salvatore Maldini. I play for Switzerland. Yes, I got Italian name, but my Mother, she is Swiss. If I leave it later, who knows, maybe I play for Italy. What? You don't believe me. You don't believe me! Is true! (*Slams the cleaver down.*) I only joke. I have a problem with the drink. It ruins my football. One day, I play for my team. Swiss team, Grasshoppers. Very good team. You don't believe me? (*Slams the cleaver down.*) Now you believe me? Good. We are playing in the Swiss cup verses Interlaken – Interlaken shit. I'm with a big headache. Night before I'm drinking too much. It's five minutes to go and I'm defending a corner, when the ball comes I think, I head this, this hurt my head. But I do this for my team. You don't believe me? Is true! I head, we go up field. Enzo slip ball to Lantini. (*Conspiratorially.*) Lantini – big wanker... Anyway, Lantini send a crossfield ball to Grun. Grun down the wing like his arse on fire. Cross. Who is there? Salvatore. Bullet in back of the net. We win. Salvatore big hero... What? You don't believe me! You don't believe me!!! Is true! What? What? You never heard of me? Huh! Only reason you don't see my name on World Cup teamsheet is because I have terrible injury

when I get to '66 World Cup. Big training ground accident.
Otherwise you all know me… Broken leg in training.
Compound fracture from team mate. Wanker Lantini!
(*Long pause. He sits, takes a drink.*)
You think I drink too much sherry? You think I drink too
much sherry!!! This is not sherry! This is sherry bottle fill
with Jack Daniels! I don't drink sherry! You like? Huh?
You like? Maybe you should eat my trifle! Amos! Where is
Amos? Amos, bring trifle!
(*SALVATORE exits. AMOS enters with trifle. He offers a portion
to a member of the audience (if possible it should be drenched in
Jack Daniels). AMOS is a thin Nigerian man of about thirty.*)

AMOS: There was once a man who had no trifle. His name
was Sylvester. One day Sylvester broke into a warehouse.
The warehouse belonged to Mr Falana. Mr Falana was
a very rich man. He was an importer and exporter. In
Mr Falana's warehouse were many wonderful and exotic
things: kaleidoscope-coloured butterflies from South
America; polar animal skins from the Antarctic; hand
made carpets from Istanbul; ancient manuscripts from
the libraries of Athens and Rome; luminous seashells
from the Caribbean. All on their way from somewhere
to somewhere. So never long in Mr Falana's warehouse.
Sylvester he had worked for Mr Falana for many years, but
he was very poor. Every night when he came home from
work his wife would ask him what he had brought for their
supper. And every night he would produce the handful of
millet his meagre earnings would allow him to buy. And
every night his wife and children would cry and his wife
would beg him to ask for a pay rise. And so it happened
that one morning Sylvester went to his boss' office. 'Mr
Falana,' said Sylvester to his boss, 'I have worked for you
for fifteen years, but in all those years you have never
given me even one pay rise.' 'Pay rise!' exclaimed Mr
Falana. 'What do you want with a pay rise! Don't I let you
see the beautiful butterflies from the Amazon; don't I let
you read the Sanskrit manuscripts from India; don't I let
you stroke the skin of the Siberian Tiger?' 'But Mr Falana,'
pleaded Sylvester, 'my family is starving.' Mr Falana was
sad. He looked into his warehouseman's yellowed eyes.

'Then you must find another job Sylvester,' he said. And he turned away. That night when Sylvester came home his wife and children were sitting by the empty cooking pot waiting for him. 'What have you bought for our supper tonight, Sylvester,' asked his wife. And just as he did every night Sylvester dug deep into his frayed trouser pocket and pulled out a handful of millet. His wife looked sorrowfully at the grain. 'Husband,' she said sadly, 'surely we will all starve. Tomorrow you must promise me you will ask for a pay rise.' Sylvester hung his head. 'I went to Mr Falana this morning,' he explained, ' and now I must find another job.' For ten days and ten nights Sylvester searched for work. But there were no jobs to be had. For ten days and ten nights Sylvester, his wife and his six children starved. Then, one afternoon, as Sylvester walked through the market he saw some sweet cassava lying in the gutter. He paused to pick up the cassava which he put in his pocket. But a policeman had seen Sylvester and Sylvester was arrested and taken to see a judge. Now, it so happened that the judge's nephew was a trader in the market who made his living from selling tapioca made from the root of the cassava and he was not kindly disposed to Sylvester. 'You are an evil man,' said the judge. 'You will go to prison for twenty years.' In the truck on the way to jail a man who had murdered his father-in-law told Sylvester of the great earnings to be had in a country across the sea, where money could be made by the shirtfull. And so it was that Sylvester decided he must escape to this land and earn money to send back to his family. That very same night Sylvester scaled the wall of the prison with the tied shirts of fifty men and ran through the cover of darkness to the docks where he sneaked through a hole in the fence into the warehouse of Mr Falana. In the pitch blackness he found a large packing crate. He prised open the lid and climbed inside. Then he nailed himself in and fell into a deep, deep sleep. When Sylvester awoke, he could hear the stomach rumble of near-by turbines and feel the roll of the sea. Soon, he thought to himself, soon I will be in the new land and my family will eat. But hour after hour passed and the ship did not dock. And Sylvester was becoming

very hungry. Through a crack in the wooden crate a thin
sheet of light illuminated many packages, each wrapped in
coloured paper or cloth and bound for the land across the
sea. Sylvester pulled at the string of one of the packages
and the primrose coloured sugar paper slid gently down to
reveal a lepidopterist's tray; under the glass were pinned
the wings of a hundred brightly coloured butterflies and
moths. For many hours Sylvester stared at the beautiful
creatures until his stomach began once again to cry out in
hunger to him. Try as he may Sylvester could not make
the hunger go away. Before his eyes the butterflies became
fowl and the moths game. Carefully, he slid the glass
from the case and one by one plucked the wings from the
lepidoptra, placed them on his tongue and swallowed.
And for a while his hunger was satisfied. But the hours still
passed and Sylvester once again became hungry. Now he
turned to the other packages. And so as day followed day
Sylvester survived by eating expensive fabrics from the
orient; slippers with coiled toes from Arabia; reindeer skins
from Lapland; the words of ancient philosophers; and
the cogs and springs of cuckoo clocks from Switzerland.
Until, at long last, the boat docked in the land across the
sea and Sylvester slipped from the hold to the shore of
this promised land. But the people of this country did not
like Sylvester to be there. 'We have problems of our own!'
they yelled at him. 'We have our own families to feed.' So
they locked Sylvester up in their prisons while their judges
decided what to do. After many appeals Sylvester was let
go. And he soon found work waiting tables. He was happy
to send home his money. But the authorities were not
happy that Sylvester worked, they told him he cannot do
this and they locked him once again in their prisons. And
now Sylvester's heart is broken, because far away across
the sea he knows his wife and children are starving. But he
is frightened to go back. And he is frightened to stay.
(*AMOS takes a butterfly from his pocket. He plucks off the wings
and places them on his tongue. (Perhaps he could offer wings
– coloured rice paper – to members of the audience?) He exits.
Enter MARGARET. MARGARET is a middle-aged Londoner; she
is BRIAN's wife. As she tells her story she swigs from a bottle*

of mineral water. She waves a photograph of a very overweight man – BRIAN.)

MARGARET: (*Showing the photo.*) See that… Brian McLeish at twenty-five and a half stone. My husband. Runs this place. Disaster area. (*Takes a swig of water.*) No ordinary mineral water this, you know. No… This is from the well in the back garden. And in about twenty years from now this will be the most valuable lifesource in the northern hemisphere. Let me tell you why. Over the past four years the amount of annual rainfall in Europe has dropped by 32.7%. At that rate, in a few years time, it will no longer be raining at all, anywhere on this continent. Soon what little water remains will be polluted and poisonous, the juice will have been sucked from everything that juice can be sucked from, blood will have been let to the point of self-induced mass anaemia, bladders will have shrivelled up and the world will have become the plague-ridden Mad Max-esque domain of marauding dry-mouthed pirates and bandits. (*Takes a swig.*) True. In Britain disease will sweep through the population like a sandstorm, totally decimating it. It's bound to happen. The sores of the afflicted will produce the first moisture people will have seen in years and there'll be no police force left to stop people going about licking the lesions of the dead and dying in an attempt to whet their parched lips and cardboard tongues. You mark my words. Then, at our lowest ebb, me and Brian will remember the old well in the back garden. We'll stagger out the house across the dust bowl that was once our vegetable patch, lift the slabs shoved across the well in 1986 to keep the kids out and lower a plastic bucket on a piece of old washing line. When the washing line's all gone, we'll tie on the flex from our lawn mower extension cable. When the extension cable's fully extended, we'll tie on our withered garden hose. When the hose is stretched to it's limit, we'll knot on the string we used to use to tie up the tomatoes. When the string's all unravelled, we'll tie on our shoe laces. Then, somewhere deep beneath us there'll be this barely perceptible… (*Quietly.*) Splash!… We'll look at each other, hoist up the bucket and, hey presto, there it'll be…a sploshing bucket of pure mineral water. And we

will drink. God, how we'll drink. And our bladders will
unshrivel and we'll piss again, for the first time in years.
And it'll be bloody painful, but we'll be grateful. And do
you know what, as all around us die, we'll get healthier
and healthier. Until one day, bandits will notice the runner
beans growing in the back garden and demand to know
the source of our water so that their rebel army may
drink. And we'll say, 'Bollocks!' And me and Brian will
be exposed to brutal torture and humiliation. Eventually
Brian will crack and tell them the location of the well. But
I'll trick them. They'll lower the bucket, but when they
pull it up it'll be empty and they'll declare the well dry
and move on to torture some other poor unfortunate sod.
How so? Because, being a clever so-and-so, I'll have put
pin pricks in the bottom of the bucket so that by the time
the bandits have hoisted it up the water'll have drip drip
dripped back out again. Clever, eh. After that Brian'll
always call me his Dear Liza. You know, (*From the song.*)
'There's a hole in my bucket, Dear Liza, Dear Liza...' And
so we'll resume our life of mineral water and bliss. But
the day'll come when we're the only people left on the
planet. A kind of withered Adam and Eve. And we'll fall
out over whose turn it is to water the sprouts. And Brian'll
get in a foul temper and banish me from the house. 'I
could die out here!' I'll scream at him, but he won't care.
Heartbreaking it'll be. Then, after a few days, he'll get ill.
But he won't let me help. I'll beg him, but he won't let
me in and I'll be too week to get over the fence round the
back. Eventually though, he will open the door. And he'll
say he's sorry. He'll tell me the real reason he chucked
me out was because the well was dry and he wanted the
last drop of water for himself. He'll be in a right state.
He'll say sorry over and over and, eventually, I'll forgive
him. Because I'm like that. Then he'll die. And I'll start to
cry. But no tears'll come, of course. I'll go out in the back
garden, lower the patched up bucket down the well and
heave up nothing but dust. Then I'll feel this splash, just
here. (*Touches her cheek.*) And I'll look up to the heavens and
I'll feel another. And another. And it'll start to rain. And I'll

remember Brian lying dead in the house, and I'll think to myself, serves the bastard right.

(*MARGARET takes a swig. She exits. SALVATORE enters.*)

SALVATORE: You remember pop group Brotherhood Of Man? Big pop group from 1970's. Eurovision Song Contest. I am the fat one with the moustache in this pop group. You don't believe me? Is true!

(*Slams down his cleaver. He pauses. Takes a drink.*)

You know that taxi driver win *Mastermind*. This is me. Is true! Jesus, tell them is true. Jesus!

(*SALVATORE exits. JESUS enters. JESUS is a Brazillian kitchen assistant in his mid twenties. He has a large silver salver on which are slivers of fruit. As he tells his story he offers the fruit to those listening.*)

JESUS: Every summer Juliana Santos and her family would harvest the oranges from her orange grove and celebrate the new fruit with a party. But her son, Jesus, would always stay in his room. Because Jesus Santos could not bear the sight of bright oranges. After the oranges were harvested, Juliana Santos would peel the plumpest fruit and soak the flesh for three days and nights in sugarwater and honey. On the fourth day Juliana Santos would serve the oranges in their delicious marinade to all the children of the village. All the children except her son, Jesus, who could not bear the taste and would sit at the side of the road his head turned away in disgust and his ears blocked to the sound of the poor village children as they sucked and slurped on Juliana Santos' fabulous sugarhoney orange. The feasting over, Juliana Santos would dry the skins of her oranges on the step of her house. But Jesus, her son, did not like the smell of orange peel so she was forced to dry the skins only when he was at school. From the dried orange peel Juliana Santos made laces for her children's sandals. But her son, Jesus, did not like to touch the stretched and plaited peel so he always walked about with his sandals undone. One day, when he was sixteen, Jesus decided that he must leave his village. He knew he could never be contented where the soil was dead to all but the orange grove. And so with the bittersweet tang of his mother's kiss fresh on his lips Jesus set off. At a crossroads on the dusty track that led out of the village Jesus Santos saw an old man sitting cross-legged beneath a broken signpost. 'Old man,' said Jesus, 'I am leaving my village and do not know which road to take.' The old man looked at him. With a crooked finger he pointed North. 'That way,' he said, 'lies the village of Alvares, where they harvest the finest Grapefruit in all the Americas. To the East, is San Vicente where the streets are lined with the lemon and lime. And to the West is Pavao where they grow the small, succulent kumquat and where they sew the sweet-smelling rinds together to make clothes more fine and delicate than the Chinese make from the silkworm.' Jesus thanked the old man and turned West to Pavao. He had always loved fine clothes and was eager to taste the kumquat. But Jesus was disappointed. For the kumquat tasted like the vile sugarhoney orange and the clothes tore at the slightest catch. So he travelled back East along the track to the crossroads and the old man waved as Jesus passed by. It was dark when Jesus arrived in the village of San Vicente. He booked himself a room in the village hotel and fell into a deep sleep, almost drugged by the powerful aroma of lemon and lime. He awoke to the barking cicadas in the bright light of the next morning to find his skin covered in strange green and yellow ellipses. As he ran to the village doctor he became almost asphyxiated by the overpowering smell of the lemon and lime lined avenues. The old doctor looked at Jesus with a tear in his eye. 'I have seen this only once before,' he said. 'A beautiful young girl. Not much older than you. She came to visit with her Aunt. On the day she arrived everyone remarked how the scent from the lemons and the limes was greater than anyone could remember. This very morning, my wife remarked upon the keen-scentedness of the air as we drank our lime juice. I fear you may be afflicted by the same disease.' 'What is it?' Jesus pleaded. 'What will happen to me?' 'The disease is called Leonella's Ellipses, after the girl who died.' 'She died!' 'You have a fatal allergy to the citruses of our village. Your only chance is to leave now.' So Jesus left the village of San Vicente. And he was fortunate, for with every step he took, the strange ellipses faded. Soon Jesus found himself back at the crossroads. He turned sharp right in the direction of Alvares. Jesus was welcomed into the village and that night he drank grapefruit wine and ate grapefruit escallops with the locals in the village square. And Jesus was very happy. At last, he thought to himself, this is where I belong. The years passed, Jesus made many friends and became an important man in Alvares. And he was very proud when one day the head of the village called him to his house. He told Jesus that the fertile lands around Alvares were producing the best grapefruit his people had ever known, but the fruit had become so popular there was now not enough to meet the demand. 'We must find new lands to plant our trees,' said the head of the village. And Jesus agreed that he was the man to find and cultivate these lands. First he travelled to the village of San Vicente, where he uprooted the kumquat trees and planted the grapefruit in their place. Next he journeyed to Pavao, where he rested on the outskirts of the village while his men burned the lemon and lime trees. All that remained was to return to his home village. At the crossroads the old man asked Jesus if he had found contentment. And Jesus replied that he was content. 'And today,' he pronounced, 'I will ride my horse into my mother's village and plant the first grapefruit tree in my very own family's orchard.' The old man shook his wrinkled head and said sadly, 'But surely you understand the grapefruit will never grow there.' Jesus laughed and told him the grapefruit tree was strong enough to grow in any soil. And with that he rode off into the familiar sights of his childhood. Juliana Santos was overjoyed to see her son. She wept as she embraced him and called all her many grandchildren to see their uncle. But the happiness was not to last long. For Jesus took an axe to the orange grove and the oranges were burned to a blackened pulp. 'Why?' cried Juliana Santos. 'Because now you and all the people of my birthplace must learn to eat the grapefruit,' replied her son. But year after year the grapefruit harvest failed in his mother's village. The people there grew angry and many refused to eat the grapefruit imported from Alvares. Jesus was furious and ordered these villagers to be put to death. In desperation, Juliana Santos came to her son and begged him to stop the brutal killings, but he was deaf to her pleas. And so Juliana Santos walked from the village to the crossroads to ask the old man what she should do. 'You must visit the doctor in San Vicente,' the old man told her, 'he will know what you must do.' That night, after speaking with the doctor, Juliana Santos slipped into Jesus' home and in the bedroom beneath Jesus' pillow she placed a single lemon and a single lime. The following morning Jesus awoke to find the strange green and yellow ellipses returned to his skin. Within three hours his body was ablaze with sores the colour of gold and seaweed. And that night, with skin the texture of lemon and colour of lime, he passed away. In time Juliana Santos returned to growing her oranges. Today, in San Vicente, the lemon and lime trees once again line the streets. And in Pavao the kumquat grows more succulent than ever. But as the old man will tell you if you stand at the crossroads, no lesson has been learned.

(*JESUS exits. PATRICIA enters. PATRICIA is an American woman in her mid-twenties. Her story is delivered as a lecture (with lectern, notes and diagrams – maybe use Powerpoint). As she talks she intermittently itches, scatches and swats at imagined insects.) Offers audience a snack from a tub of maggots?*)

PATRICIA: Thank you. Hi. My name is Dr Patricia Margoles and I'm from the University of Michigan, Chicago. I'm here today to talk to you about Bugman or what you in Britain call the Insectiverous Entomosapien. First of all, who or what is Bugman? Well, for starters just think about all those little cuts and bruises and insect bites you get and you don't know how you got them…chances are they coulda been made by Bugman. This, (*Shows a diagram – a rough sketch of the half man/half insect bugman.*) is a drawing made by seventeen year old Lucy Webb from Birmingham, England. Notice the compound eyes and the arthropod-like, horny shell beneath the wings on Bugman's back. Lucy Webb's case is not a unique one, but she is one of only three individuals to have woken during an attack and actually survive. She is the only one to survive and remain sane. Now, Lucy was not a particularly entomophobic child. Sure, she had a thing about spiders and maggots and she wasn't that keen on earwigs, but she was no more phobic than any other child growing up in the UK during the 1970s and 80s. So why her? Why, indeed. We may never know. But on the evening of 17th November 1986, three weeks after her seventeenth birthday, Lucy went to bed early after watching an episode of the UK soap *Coronation Street.* That night at around four in the morning she was awoken by the sound of what she describes as sheets of sandpaper being rubbed together, or, as she later put it more onomatopoeically – (*Rubs her hands together to illustrate.*) shh shh, shh shh, shh shh, shh shh. She informs us in her first book *I Was A Teenage Insectiverous Entomosapien* that she had woken up when she felt her face brushed by a gossamer-like fabric. That 'fabric' turned out to be Bugman's wings and when she opened her eyes this (*The drawing.*) is what she saw standing over her. Now, what is it Bugman does exactly, you ask. Good question. Does he just pinch and scratch us? No. What Lucy saw as Bugman gripped her arms, thus bruising and scratching her, was an army of arthropods – spiders, centipedes, etc (*Shows pictures.*) – annelids – earthworms, roundworms, etc (*Shows pictures.*) – dipterous insects – flies, etc (*Shows picture.*) – insects of the hymenopterous family – white ants, red ants, termites (*Shows picture.*) – she saw an army of these creatures pouring from Bugman's mouth, nose and eye sockets as he bent to kiss her. She panicked. But she found that as the insects and worms dropped onto her face and into her own mouth, she was unable to scream. Fortunately, as fate would have it, at that very moment Lucy's insomniacal mom got out of bed to visit the bathroom. She switched on the landing light and in a blind panic, Bugman threw up his wings and flew out the open window. Now Lucy could scream, and boy did she scream. Her mom came running in to see Lucy thrashing at the ants and maggots crawling in her hair. Fortunately Lucy's mom, a lady of West Indian origin, was not easily fazed and she soon had the situation under control. Over the past fourteen years there have been seventy-two reports of Bugman attacks. All but three were fatal. All victims were found crawling with insects. There have been reports of attacks all over the world. In South America a dead girl's mouth was prised open by a curious surgeon two days after she had been medically fumigated and a squadron of flying ants flew out into his face. In Australia, a train of funnel webs crawled from the large intestine of a young woman during an autopsy almost three weeks after her death. The majority of victims are literally eaten from the inside out. One or two of them a mere insect bitten shell by the time the bugs have finished. From Lucy Webbs' sketches of Bugman, here reproduced in her second book *Return Of Bugman* (*Shows sketches.*) and details picked up from research in and around the West Midlands and the Home Counties of England, Bugman's prime stomping ground, I was able to begin building up a profile of the insect man. Then, on a visit to Surrey University, Guildford, Surrey last May, I heard an incredible story. An old man rang the Zoology Department and asked to speak with me. I met him in the Crown and Thistle Public House. (*Shows picture.*) Lionel Brown, the elderly gentleman in question, had read about my research in the Sunday Sport and he told me the story, told to him by his grandfather, of a man called Wilfred Pink. Mr Pink had been a poacher living in the late nineteenth century in the village of Effingham. At the time, the lord of Effingham manor was a man by the name of William Docherty, and Mr Docherty was heartily sick of the poachers on his land. To teach Wilfred Pink a lesson Docherty and his gamekeeper set man traps around the estate. On the night of 17th November 1882 Wilfred Pink put his foot in one of the traps and was found next morning, his leg severed at the ankle dragging himself through Docherty's woodlands by Docherty and his gamekeeper. They didn't help Wilfred, they just laughed callously and left him to crawl home. But Wilfred Pink never made it home. He fell in a ditch and died there, his body crawling with maggots, gnawed and eaten by a thousand different species of insect. Exactly a year later, Docherty's two daughters started finding insect bites, odd bruises and scratch marks on their arms and legs. And two years to the day after Pink's agonising death both girls were found dead in their beds, their bodies crawling with centipedes, worms, spiders and wasps. Mr Brown showed me a photograph (*She scratches herself.*) of Wilfred Pink. (*Shows photo and holds up next to it a sketch of the bugman's face.*) See the likeness. Sweet dreams.

(*PATRICIA exits. Enter SALVATORE. He slams down his cleaver.*)

SALVATORE: Gordon Ramsay… Wanker!

(*SALVATORE exits. A moment later CLAIRE enters from outside. CLAIRE is a thirty-something, Mancunian food and drink critic. She finds herself a table and sits down. During her monologue CLAIRE nibbles on a carrot. After a brief pause she takes out her mobile and punches in a number.*)

CLAIRE: (*Into her mobile.*) Trevor, it's Claire…some dive called the International Café… I know it's near, that's why I thought I'd give you a bell…me too, darling… No idea. Why don't you come over…go on… I can't leave, I've only just got here… Trevor… Oh, be like that then… (*Puts the phone away. notices audience.*) Is it me? Oh sorry… (*Clears throat.*) I love my work. My two favourite things. Writing, and eating and drinking. Three. My three favourite things. That's why I do it. Food and drink critic. Quite a laugh. Did a piece for the *Observer* couple of weeks ago. Just a little bit. They put it in next to Nick Cohen. Might get some more work from it. Fingers crossed. I write for *The Guardian* mainly. I like to be jokey, colourful, colloquial, take the piss a bit. Like to think of my readers as my mates. You know. An easy kind of style, like you just got home from the pub and you want to tell your flatmate about how many pints you drank and who was there. Play a few word games, food-word games. Make up a few quips, that kind of thing. Entertain. Be witty. I think of myself as an entertainer. My readers don't read me just for information. No. They get that. The information. But they get entertained as well. Food and drink criticism isn't just about what's on the plate, it's about the ambience, it's about the people, it's about the last time Nicole Kidman ate there. It's a living thing. An eating, drinking, thinking, feeling, experiencing it thing. A real thing. I want it to be a tactile almost fetishistic experience for the men and women who read me. I provide a service. It's important

work. People take notice of what I say. Some people get
a bit angry with me, but what can you do? I speak as I
see. I write as I taste. And if it tastes shit, then I say it.
Shit. I've had some furious phone calls from besmirched
restaurateurs. And hate mail. God! I am fair. People want
to know what I think. I'm not going to lie. My reputation's
on the line. If I say some place is great and a *Guardian*
reader goes there and it's shite, it's my face in the kack. My
word as well as their maple glazed chicken wings down
the toilet. But something's been bothering me a bit lately.
I think… Well, I don't know how, but some very strange
things have been happening. Three weeks ago a colleague
of mine went to a seafood place in London, I can't name
names but it's next door to the newsagents on Frith Street
in Soho. Anyway, in his review – he didn't like the place,
but he didn't dislike it – in his review he had a go about
the lobster: '…submerged beneath a spermatozoa gloop
of mayonnaise, pepper and lemon, this lobster looked
like it had just crawled into the restaurant after a nasty
accident at the local sperm bank.' Well, that's not horrible,
is it? My God, though, the owner went ballistic. E-mails,
letters, phone calls. And Malcolm, that's his name, poor
old Malcolm. Well, it all starts to get to him. There's not
a minute of the day when he's not being harassed by
this bloke. He had to take out a court order to keep him
away. Reckoned Malcolm had singlehandedly ruined
his business. Stupid man. Thing was, this was when the
really weird stuff started. It was his hands first. (*She does an
imitation of opening and closing lobster claws.*) 'Stop doing that
with you hands, Malcolm,' I'd say to him. 'Doing what?'
he'd reply. Hadn't noticed. And then his eyes started going
real beady and before you know it he's crawling about on
all fours eating nothing but crabsticks. Then it happened.
It was on the BBC. Bright red, he was when they found
him. Scalded himself to death in a bathful of boiling hot
water. And that's not the only weird thing. Another of my
colleagues referred to some fuck-off-expensive chicken in a
Mayfair eaterie as an insult to Bernard Matthews. Two days
later she pulled all her hair out, basted herself in Flora and
fried to death under her own sunlamp. Yes, and during the

autopsy they found one and a half kilograms of chestnut stuffing inserted into her colon. Scarry stuff. I just wish I hadn't had a go at that Braised Rabbit I had in Quo Vadis last week… (*Her mobile rings.*) Yes… Trevor… I can't… Do you?… Do you really?… All right… I said, all right… Just some lettuce and carrots for me… Yes, see you… (*Puts her phone away.*) Got to run…

(*CLAIRE exits. SALVATORE enters. He goes to say something. Stops. And exits. Enter ANDRIS. ANDRIS is a down-and-out. He is in his mid-thirties and comes from Latvia. He takes off his filthy greatcoat.*)

ANDRIS: Andris Ulmanis-Ambramkhin got a job washing dishes in the kitchen of the most expensive and famous French restaurant in Riga. Andris did not like people. He preferred the company of the rain and sun and he slept out in all weathers under the trees and awnings of Riga's streets. He was content and happy to be on his own in a world where he understood the coming and going of the day and night, the dogs and insomniacs, sailors and prostitutes. At the restaurant Andris talked to no one and no one talked to him, but he was the best kitchen orderly in Riga and was respected for his hard work and punctuality. Andris was paid only a small amount for his work and always looked gaunt and starving, but one of the waiters took pity and began to fill Andris' coat pockets with succulent leftovers from the tables of the wealthy who ate at Riga's most expensive and famous French restaurant. Always sending him away with far more than he could ever eat. And so it was that this man who slept on the streets grew healthy and strong and looked well from eating so much fine food. And soon the street people of Riga came to hear about the good fortune that Andris had found and they would follow him from bench to bench, shop doorway to underground passageway, through the city's midnight streets to beg the juicy scraps from his pockets. The demand for the leftovers became so great that each evening queues would form and snake along the street where Andris would always come after work to sit on his favourite bench. Soon Andris was being offered money and favours for his food. Before long his

boots and socks were stuffed with roubles and he had
many friends. Andris did not have an idle mind and his
thoughts turned to what he might do with his money. First
he took a room in a small hostel, but the smell of soap
and clean linen was too much for a man used to Riga's
concrete and belching chimneys. So he bought himself
a bicycle. But Andris missed the feel on the pavement
beneath his feet and the bicycle always got him to places
too soon. Then, one day, the manager of the restaurant
stopped Andris on his way out after work and searched
his coat pockets. He was furious to discover escargot, wild
mushrooms and envelopes of filo pastry filled with goats
cheese and avacado. Andris was dismissed on the spot.
When his friends heard that Andris had been dismissed
and that he could no longer feed them they deserted him.
Andris decided he must use what remained of his money
sensibly and bought a motorised falafel van. It was very
old and dirty, but Andris scrubbed and scoured until the
van was clean and gleaming and ready. Andris had learned
many tricks from watching the great chefs in the kitchen
of Riga's most expensive and famous French restaurant
and was soon cooking the finest food to be eaten on the
streets. Soon, even regulars from the expensive and famous
French restaurant preferred to stop off at the roadside
and eat Andris Ulmanis-Ambramkhin's moules and duck.
Then, one day, Andris returned to the restaurant where
the owner was sitting alone crying into his upturned palms.
Andris bought the restaurant from him for a very fair
price and soon the most expensive and famous French
restaurant in Riga was precisely that again. But Andris
was not happy. He missed the parks and the trees and
the cats and pigeons. He was tired of the company of
adoring friends. He was worn out by the comfort of his
waterfront penthouse. All he wanted was to put on his
boots and walk the streets again. But Andris was famous.
Everybody in Riga knew him and he could go nowhere
without being recognised and mobbed. The solitude and
anonymity he craved were as out of reach to him now as
riches and comforts had once seemed. But one night, a
tramp banged on the window of the kitchen where Andris

was supervising his staff. Andris invited him in and soon recognised the man as the waiter who many years ago had given the scraps to him. They embraced. The waiter told him how he had been dismissed when it was discovered he was responsible for giving the leftovers to Andris. He asked Andris for his old job back and Andris at once agreed. Then Andris had an idea. And the following day he disappeared. All he left was a letter detailing his wish that the restaurant be handed over to the waiter. From that day to this no one has seen Andris. One rumour has it that he was murdered and served up in his own restaurant, but Andris has written many letters to his friend the waiter since his disappearance with ideas for new recipes. Another rumour suggests that he has gone to Moscow to be an advisor in President Putin's kitchen. A third is that he fled the country and resumed his old lifestlye in a foreign land. Perhaps this could explain the waiter's many trips to feed the down and outs in Britain. *(He pulls on his coat.)* We may never know.

(ANDRIS exits. BRIAN enters. As he winds up the evening he becomes more and more desperate.)

BRIAN: Ladies and Gents, thank you very much for coming. I hope you've enjoyed the food...stories. I trust you found them nourishing. It certainly made my mouth water...just to think of all that...food. All kinds of wonderful food. From crisps and crudités to soufflé and sauerkraut. Chocolate and cheeses. Cornflakes, ice cream, duck, chicken, beef, vegetable roulade, sausages... Oh God, I love sausages. And bacon. Sautéed potatoes... Chips, waffles, boiled, baked, mashed. Oh God. Oh God. I can't stand it!

(BRIAN rushes about the restaurant retrieving hidden and stashed snacks: Curley Wurleys sellotaped underneath chairs; packets of crisps hidden in light fittings; sausage rolls hidden in plant pots, etc. When he is piled high with food, he turns back to the audience.)

(Looks at the food in his hands.) Win some, lose some. The restaurant's open. They've got real food. Real, glorious, edible, digestible... Better hurry, though. I'm starving...
(End.)